GRASPING

For Alexander

For a common kindness
(The Qur'an, Sura 107)

GRASPING AFRICA
A Tale of Tragedy and Achievement

Stephen Chan

I.B. TAURIS

LONDON · NEW YORK

Published in 2007 by I.B.Tauris & Co Ltd
6 Salem Road, London W2 4BU
www.ibtauris.com

In the United States and in Canada distributed by Palgrave
Macmillan a division of St Martin's Press, 175 Fifth Avenue, New
York NY 10010

ISBN 978 1 84511 285 1

A full CIP record for this book is available from the British Library
A full CIP record is available from the Library of Congress

Library of Congress Catalog card: available

Typeset in Berkeley Oldstyle by Oxford Publishing Services, Oxford
Printed and bound in Great Britain by TJ International Ltd, Padstow,
Cornwall

Contents

Preface

It is not red, perhaps rusty, but many tanks lie covered by the water – just as many chariots were said to have been drowned further up the coastline. It is early 1993, the eve of independence for Eritrea. I stand on a beach overlooking the Red Sea. Behind me are the ruins of Massawa. I am reminded of the Biblical expression, 'not a stone shall be left standing on a stone'; every building in the city has been bombed into ruins. I am recovering for the drive back up the mountains to Asmara. Back at the Landcruiser the minders are conjecturing how well, or badly, I took their latest spectacle. To illustrate the cruelty of the Dergue's regime, I was shown an execution ground. I'd say about 600 bodies – their remains, that is. I say to myself, 'well, Stephen, here we are at last, inducted into atrocity tourism,' except that after 13 years of trudging all over Africa I'd pretty much seen the lot. It's usually presented with a little less showmanship, that's all.

I walk along the beach, out of the sight of my minders. I should have taken my shirt, I'm burning a rusty red, I fall into step with a teenage boy and we let the waves wash our feet as we walk together. He speaks English. 'I am here to mourn my brother, who fell in the battle for Massawa.' It had been a ferocious battle. The Eritrean liberation forces had thrown suicide attacks against the Soviet tanks. After they had won the city, a wing of MIG fighter-bombers dropped phosphorous bombs on Massawa for a week. Those who emerged must have thought they were invulnerable. The boy's brother had not emerged. 'You are English.' I put my arm around him. It's not often I am taken as English on first sight. 'Ten years ago, there was terrible famine here. I was a child then. I am told that, in your country, England, there was a singer who tried to help us.'

That was all I needed. Skeletal corpses, battlefields, bombed-out cities – they can all be filtered through a cultivated jaded-ness. You earn that jadedness. It allows you to contemplate Africa without crying. But it makes the world of Europe where you live, and the world of Africa where you have spent so much time, two very different places. As it was, I was then living in the seventeenth-century Kentish port of Faversham. Geldoff was almost a neighbour. I used to run past his con-verted church house every Sunday when I took my impossibly long run along the Saxon shoreway. But the boy's comment was what I needed to let the tears run through. Only connect. And the tousle-haired, loudmouthed lout of a musician had connected.

It is 2005 as I write this. He's at it again. He's wearing designer suits now, but he's still as loudmouthed as ever. Now he's wanting to change the whole way of thinking that the G8 has had towards Africa. No one can say the man lacks ambition. He's persuaded Tony Blair to establish a Com-mission for Africa. The people who work for it are very earnest. There's going to be a huge concert in Hyde Park and tens of thousands will come. Few will know that, in Africa, Tony Blair is the most despised British prime minister of all time. If his hectoring tone, his self-righteous certitude, his complete lack of an intellectual core, make him a wearying burden for the British people, he is seen as the personification of the condescencion that colonial rule inflicted in Africa. In Africa the raw wounds of racism are still very livid. Few in Europe can understand how deeply they run and are still felt. All we need now is for this man, Blair, to say he is leading the way for Africa, to lecture Africa, and to say it is he who will deliver them. I rather think that I shall not encounter someone on a future Eritrean beach who will tell me that a British prime minister tried to help them.

Not that it is likely that for me there will be another Eritrean beach. I had gone there to help the victorious liberation forces establish a working government. 'This is how you structure a Ministry of Foreign Affairs. ... This is what the first delegation of the IMF, coming to visit you next week, will say.' My friends in Eritrea, those who had fought the Soviet-officered armies of the Ethiopian Dergue, had been heroes and had been impossibly idealistic and hopeful, are now rotting in jail – without charge and without any prospect of a release date. Another government turned intolerant. Another set of democratic values turned to tyranny. Oh, much of great moment is still happening in Eritrea. But you get betrayed once too often, and this Chinese Englishman is not going back just yet.

At the moment of the G8 summit in Gleneagles I am writing this short book to try to decipher the terrible ambiguities of Africa, to decipher what the policy-makers say, what the Commission for Africa says, what the international civil society groups say, what the scholars say, to try to decipher what I think after 25 years of travelling, working and, off and on, living in Africa. You get jaded, but this is because you have fallen in love with a continent that consistently disappoints you. The jadedness allows you to get on with your life in Europe, but it also allows you to keep loving Africa.

And it's a hard continent to love. All 53 countries, disparate, exotic even to one another, emit a common capacity for joy and disappointment. It's winter in Zimbabwe. This Preface is being written as a brief British heat wave comes to its end. The British tennis hopes have been smashed out of Wimbledon. The British Lions are being crushed at rugby by the mighty New Zealand All Blacks. The rain, and mud, have washed into the Glastonbury music festival – and all is as it should be in the understatements and wry 'what did you expect' inflections of irony that make up the impossible creole of Celtic, Latin, Saxon, Norman and Norse languages that now passes as English; a patois that is in love with ironies, conditionals and politesses, and which all the world takes to be hypocritical and perfidious – including in Africa, and particularly in Zimbabwe. But, as the gallant losers parade in their whites at the beginning of Wimbledon, the Mugabe government is smashing entire suburbs, dispossessing tens if not hundreds of thousands. And winters on the high plateau on which Harare sits can be cold indeed. Having evicted the white farmers, like Saturn, Mugabe is now eating his own children. Not a single African fellow president protests and this is, for me, an even greater disappointment than the sight of suburbs, with which I am in fact familiar, transformed into rubble. So it seemed the right time to attempt this book – to put some rubble of understanding together.

One person more than any other has helped to prepare me

for a considered effort. When I began lecturing with Donal Cruise O'Brien in 2003, I realized instantly how meagre had been my range and depth of reading on Africa. This reading had not been insignificant, but Donal's was magisterial. Moreover, week by week, he delegated our M.Sc. students to report on key texts. I owe to them insights I all too often missed in my frantic rush to catch up.

I have had many friends to thank over my quarter century engagement with Africa: Henderson Tapela, Johnson Ndlovu, Emmanuel Apea, Abdul Maman, Kwaku Osei-Hwedie, Walter Mazzuki, Francis Omondi, Demeterio Obbo-Kawaka, Raymond Mbazima, Wycliffe Mushipi, Josephine Mwale, Lloyd Chingambo, Petros Solomon, Cirino Hiteng, Tichafa Maswinge, Paul Danisa, Ranka Primorac – not all of them are still alive, but those who are will remember the impossible adventures and projects we undertook. And those who died? The usual: HIV/AIDS, car crash (accidental or engineered by political opponents), the rumour is (you lose touch) of a firing squad. The rumour says a failed uprising against corruption; it says a volume of poetry in his pocket as he faced the rifles. Another rumour says I am beguiled by reports of another officer with the same name, and that my lost friend is in fact prospering. Well, friend or unknown, whoever assumed the Byronic romance with freedom was dead in Africa? I pay respect here. I send my thoughts to Petros Solomon in an Eritrean jail; to his wife who returned to Eritrea to help him and was herself incarcerated. 'We never argue,' Petros had once drunkenly informed me. 'We never argue, my wife and I.' I politely but also drunkenly asked why? 'Because she can shoot straighter and faster than I can!' The table, I remember, dissolved into laughter. This is for all those who fought for something. Africa is more than debt tables and aid requirements. It is about something very great in the face of tragedy. We comment only on the tragedy. I would like to comment on both in this little book – while hiding neither my profound disappointments nor my continuing hopes.

Stephen Chan
Pimlico 2005

Introduction

There are 53 countries in Africa, all states or claiming to be states. If a nation corresponds to a language group there are more than 300 nations in Nigeria, about 80 in Zambia. The geographical space in Africa is immense. Kafue Game Park in Zambia is half the size of Switzerland. Western Europe fits several times over in Democratic Republic of Congo. To prevent overreach, in this book I shall make the traditional divide and deal with Africa south of the Sahara – black Africa – although this is an artificial distinction. States such as Sudan are divided between Arab and black populations. Islam is not only the predominant religion of Arab Africa but of much of the western and eastern seaboards. And it is not as if it is only in black Africa where the world's media ponders tragedy caused by natural disasters or Africans against those who seem their own. In Sudan's Darfur region, it is Arab militias who visit atrocity upon African villages; in Algeria, it is Arab violence against Arab; in the as-yet unsettled war in Western Sahara, both Polissario liberation fighters and Moroccan loyalists are Arab. And even that which is called black Africa is not fully black. There would be no lingering racialism if significant white populations did not remain, or significant interbreeding as in South Africa and the Lusophone countries. Somalia, Ethiopia and Eritrea are populated by people with black African, Arabic African and

1

Yemeni characteristics built upon more individual ones. Indian people inhabit Mauritius and the Malagasy Republic. The Phoenicians and the Chinese reached Africa well before white colonialism. As for colonialism, it left what are at least stylistic imprints: the finest Italianate designs are still reproduced in Eritrea; Francophonic flair and *savoir-faire* are easily found in Senegal; clubbable Anglophonic mannerisms abound in Ghana; and in southern Africa the white population has affected a distinctly southern hemispheric tone (an Oz/Kiwi/Laager/rugger mix) which infiltrates the rising black middle class. What is called black Africa is pluralism unmatched in any other part of the world. And no one has even bothered to count the number of local religions; although there are endless studies of how Christianity has become a key ingredient in the syncretic mixes of old and new forms of worship. And Africa is syncretic. Malawian Puritanism is Victorian in its origin, as is the 'traditional' food of maize meal. With all the vastness and mixes that arise from space and people crossing space, there are the collusions of habits and customs from different times. It is not constitutionalized. In Britain, the Queen is a collusion of different times, but she has constitutional space. Where modernity and modern constitutions left no space for African customs, a vast informal network of operational codes has embedded itself in everyday life and, even if it does not always escape regulation, frequently escapes popular censure. Space, time, and values provide a super-pluralism on top of all that which is more easily observed.

In the light of all this, any effort to divide Africa between Arab north and black south is artificial. Similarly, any effort to impose a unified analysis on Africa is doomed to failure. There is just too much going on, and a lot that is going on is indecipherable to Western eyes, ears, and taste. Why, then, even attempt this book?

There is a very real sense that Africa is a Western unity – it is united as an 'Other' that confronts Europe and its own sense of self. The effort perhaps to make Africa less Other may well be because the West now sees rising on the horizon not an exotic Other that is underdeveloped, but one that is militant and sufficiently developed to be confrontational. Better to deal with Africa now, rather than wait until both Africa *and* Islam oppose the West. In addition, Africa is precisely a unity in that, Ethiopia aside, all the continent was colonized by Europe. All the continent was given its independence by Europe. All the continent (with perhaps the exceptions of Eritrea and South Africa) is seriously economically indebted to the West. It is the West that determines the 'correct' ingredients of constitutionalism, the terms of trade, the rate of aid, the amount of compassion that might be directed towards Africa. Africa is an object in the Western gaze. What at least I want to do in this book is, even if only a little, to give some African perspective to how Africa might be viewed. This is a huge presumption for a Chinese Europhile.

The second thing I want to do in this book is to make Africa seem a less instrumentalized object. It is not a place where commissions can easily tinker. I use these terms deliberately. The Commission for Africa produced a 461-page report. Some of it is brilliant. Some of it is so hopeful, and so hopeful of so few a range of instruments, that it seems like a house of cards. A glance at the report's huge bibliography is revealing. By far the greater majority of the sources are documents written for, published by, or heavily influenced by official Western mini-tries, agencies, or financial institutions. They all inhabit a certain paradigm of economic and public administrative planning that is perhaps unavoidable, but also render the African subject as recipient and beneficiary – as an instrument to be developed by Western instrumental means. We ourselves have nothing to receive from Africa. What is missing from the bibliography is any extensive account of even Western scholarship, still less African scholarship, about Africa. The more thoughtful, reflective and, indeed, introspective views of Africa are omitted in the rush to backbone the urge to 'do something now'. So, one of the things I want to do in this book is introduce some thoughtful scholarship.

But I do not want this to be an academic book. That is probably the last thing Africa now needs. I do not want to be part of the academic industry that depends in fact on Africa being poor and Other. I am going to try to write a book that humanizes Africa. I will tell stories. And this may be my greatest impertinence. I want to write a book without categorization. My academic colleagues will accuse me of sacrificing precision and rigour. My publisher will point blank demand to know whether this is a politics book, a travel book, a memoir, or a collection of creative prose. My African friends will say I have given in to the adventurism of which they have had too much already – outsiders trooping all over the continent as if they owned it and, afterwards, claiming an ownership to its interpretation, often on the basis of 'experience' and its stories; and these stories may distort things as much as seek to humanize them. They may all be right, and the reader is warned. But I have been trying to do this for years: the number of books and other works that are, separately, scholarly or creative make of themselves a ridiculously large bibliography.

For me at least, it seems like time to unify my thoughts and gather my modes of writing.

Finally, because Africa will for a short while be the object of Western concern, and the younger generation – led not by older politicians but perhaps thankfully by older musicians – has an idealism that says something must be done, I want to say that the idealism must be prepared to absorb gross disappointments. There is much that is wrong in Africa that will take many long years to put right. A great many horrendously corrupt and brutal people will get away with it all and go laughing to their graves. The generation that replaces them may be a little more honest, but will be brash new Yankees in the slightly more equalized world. Precisely with the cancelling of debt and the possible invigoration of industry, the ecology will be further vandalized, the water tables shrink, and the wildlife reduced to picturesque miniatures. And the poor will not disappear. Beautiful huge cities will grow with white towers and flowering boulevards – and, as in Brazil and India, be surrounded by teeming tenements of every conceivable (and inconceivable) misery. And what about aspiration, pure and proper? In short, a very human Africa is what will emerge, terrifyingly imperfect. Perhaps that will be an improvement on what is now so often merely terrifying.

***

In this book I shall divide each chapter into three main parts. The first sets out an 'official' debate, drawing from policy documents, the report of the Commission for Africa, the concerns of Western-based non-governmental organizations. The second sets out the scholarly debate that, often enough, nuances if not challenges the assumptions that underlie policy. The third is where I try to write humanly, drawing indeed on my own stories, but also those of African novelists and poets. Perhaps this *mélange* will offer its own ambiguities. The idea is that they will collaborate in a project to illuminate the sometimes necessary, sometimes awful ambiguities of, yes, a beloved continent.

Chapter 1

Prologue to ambiguity: a countdown

W hy has it been necessary to have a Commission for Africa? Why has Gordon Brown, Britain's Chancellor of the Exchequer, been working so hard towards debt cancellation? Why has Tony Blair been seeking to persuade the G8 not only to cancel debt but increase aid? Why has Bob Geldof, after saying 'never again', been organizing a new form of music concert? Not the concert as aid, as pioneered by George Harrison's Concert for Bangladesh, but the concert as protest. Let the common people, especially the young people, speak. Let the older politicians (in fact not much older than Geldof) hear. Make them hear.

It is the week before Geldof's concert. Since Harrison, the generations have done it differently. Harrison had no organization or aid experience. Much of the money he raised never reached Bangladesh. But who can forget him, the first Western pop musician to be immersed in the culture of India, dressed in a white suit, weeping as he sang? They do not do compassion like George anymore. The Geldof of 1984 was not just compassion. He was anger, 'bloody fucking anger', as he might have said. He established his own aid organization, and made sure that funds got through. More than that, he raised the consciousness of an entire Western generation. By contrast, the Geldof of 2005 is plain exasperation. Learned now in the ways both of the world and of personal tragedy, he just wonders loudly why, 20 years after, Africa is still a patient under long-term death watch. In fact, it seems as if it is dying very patiently indeed – and not minding that the doctors and hospital administrators are charging for the drips and medicines, and that the health authorities are stealing everything but the bed on which it lies. He might be the loudest git in the Western world, and it is well known that he enjoys hobnobbing at mahogany tables with high men, but there is enough left in him always to make the civil servants and politicians wonder which Geldoff will turn up for their meeting – the smooth operator, not unlike Bono (they would much rather deal with Bono), or the raw-mouthed *demandeur*. It is the odd, postmodern combination of bog Irish rebel, smooth jet-setting pop celebrity, adept (when he wants to be) committee-room worker, successful businessman with homes in Kent and Chelsea, single parent of a horde of young women, and pissed-off – majorly pissed-off – witness to an ongoing atrocity. For what he sees is what the otherwise non-politicized Western young see – that the exploitation and neglect of Africa is the atrocity of our times.

And yet the young do not have to be very politicized to see other things. Even in 1984, behind the skeletal backs of the starving Ethiopians, they sensed the baleful shadow of the dictator, Mengistu. The West had barely recovered from the buffoon sadism of Uganda's Amin – and, as the 1980s aged into the 2000s, both ageing youth and new youth saw the advent of new wars, new atrocities, new dictatorships, new starvations and, above all, new and huge corruptions in Africa. It is this last phenomenon more than any other that makes old and young alike sceptical. Yes, cancel the debt. Yes, equalize the terms of trade. Give them a fair playing field. But, do not support the dictatorially corrupt and the 'democratically' corrupt by sending huge amounts of aid that will be stolen, turned into Swiss chalets, Lear jets, Mercedes limousines, palaces because mere mansions are no longer enough; nor let the sight of very fat, powerful men absurdly thinking a Dior suit can hide their over-indulgence, their wives over-shopping and over-dressed at Harrods, any longer cloud our screens. For Africa has answered the West's atrocious history towards Africa with its own spectacle of callousness, greed and inhumanity. The trouble is that both the West and the African leaders commit their atrocities against the African people. Nor is it a baton change – control of corruption and atrocity changing hands. There are just more hands grasping in the continent. African warlords fight for power and control of the diamond fields. Amsterdam traders mix the 'war diamonds' with those not from conflict zones and, hey presto, the entire shipment is no longer classified as anything to do with 'war diamonds'; it has been mixed 'clean', and no longer reeks of blood, the reported cannibalisms, ritual killings and gratuitous slaughters of Liberia. French 'peacekeepers' stood aside as the Rwandan genocide progressed, because a Hutu government might favour France more than its Tutsi predecessor which had been tilting dangerously towards Britain. A very old European rivalry could be played out, as if without European transgression, in the lost city of Kigali. The Soviets and USA had done this in the 1980s over Angola. There has been almost a half century of precedents. There will be a mood at the G8 protests that says: cancel the debt, we have made so much money out of it in interest payments anyway we are actually ahead of the game; equalize the terms of trade because what is going on is simply not fair; stand by to help with emergency aid in case of great famines and natural catastrophes; otherwise, cut and run from the continent of despair. As for the ordinary people who will be left out of Western compassion, well, Western compassion never reached them anyway; and what is reaching them is the prospect of death by HIV/AIDS, which they abet by their own cultures of silence and denial surrounding the disease and, frankly, they are, whatever we try to do, a lost generation. Lingering over 2005 will be a great, unprecedented cloud that mixes compassion and callousness. Ambiguity hangs over Africa, in large part because Africa emits ambiguity.

The day before the concert

The weather forecasters say it should be fine. Almost a quarter million are expected in Hyde Park. Most people will not be able to see a thing. Better to go to Wimbledon and hope for a seat at the women's tennis finals. Alcohol will not be allowed at Hyde Park. Champagne and strawberries will be offered as the quaint tradition of the English summer at Wimbledon. The band members gearing up for Hyde Park are admitting they understand none of the detail of aid, trade and debt. They will leave the detail to Geldof and people like Bono. They just think something very large is very unfair.

The unfairness is, however, also very large in terms of how an aid 'industry' now sets about 'helping' the destitute – or not so destitute – of Africa. Whether governmental or nongovernmental, the aid programmes must satisfy the auditors

10

back home. There have to be objectives and accomplished objectives. Each objective is costed ahead of time and project management is to keep the cost within the budget. The accountants are the important clients here. And the objectives are, in any case, devised according to 'approved' project formulae, programmes that have passed muster in the board-rooms of Oxfam or whatever. There is a great show of 'local consultation' and local involvement – but no local demand for an unorthodox, imaginative, shorten-the-steps project will pass the metropolitan scrutiny. This is what is meant by 'getting the money to the people'. It means being able to show that money was spent according to plans and budgets that auditors can say were met, namely money was not wasted. Whether it benefited the 'people' is often a second-order issue.

There may be no other way of doing it. But the immediate beneficiaries may not be the poor and needy at all. There is now, again under the 'local involvement' rubric, an entire stratum of aid-personnel who attend endless workshops. In the case of HIV/AIDS, each agency and each embassy will run its own programme, disbursing its own funds. Each programme will follow set steps. There will be a study of the scale and nature of the problem, with a search as to the best entry point for funding. There will be consultation workshops followed by training workshops. Those chosen to be trained must be given project infrastructure – which means offices and cars (these days Toyota Land Cruisers). The Land Cruisers will park out-side the luxury hotels where the workshops will be held. The trainers will fly in from the West and fly out again, perhaps on business class, and have expense accounts for their stay. Next week, the same local personnel will go to another workshop, organized by another agency, and do the same thing again.

11

They can live very well like this. Then, because there are insufficient antiretrovirals in the country anyway, very few will be saved. In any case, because enrolment on an antiretroviral programme involves Western protocols of counselling – 'you may die if you do not continue the treatment; you must give the names of all your partners; you must bring in your wife/husband and family for testing; you must talk about yourself and your behaviour, to a stranger, in a way that is culturally scandalous and indecent … or you will not receive treatment and you will die' – the reticence in coming forward is immense. Not one agency says 'let us just get this stuff out there.' There is no Geldof when it comes to the detail of how it is done – when it comes to the Western detail of how it is done.

And the detailing, the planning, often takes place without the planner having stepped foot in Africa. Another stratum of people, inhabiting government, agency and university offices, makes its living as planners for Africa. Independent consultants earn successful livelihoods in the incessant round of plans that will guarantee money is well spent as far as the accounting rules are concerned. Perhaps corruption is not always a bad thing. At least it short-circuits what often resembles a circus.

The somewhat more honest Geldof circus is gearing up in Hyde Park. Grizzled, lank pony-tailed roadies are on the scene. The sound engineers, the revolving stage specialists, the TV editors, the security people, the fence builders, the toilet providers, the first aiders, the whole motley and endless cast are there. The white-haired veterans of Geldof's generation will silently, discreetly condescend to the younger musicians; the younger will hope they do not fumble their chords in front of the legends. And, because the older generation is running the show, no miming will be allowed. A lot of bum notes are going to be hit. But Geldof was always a crap musician anyway.

The concert

The concert was a great success. The one in Philadelphia was even more so. Berlin and Paris were good; but Tokyo, Moscow, Rome, Canada and Johannesburg were not that well attended. They got good stadium crowds, but Philadelphia got 400,000, and Hyde Park got close to its quarter-million target. The most elegant of African ghettoes – the concert reserved for actual African musicians, and that only as an after thought – in the beautiful gardens of Cornwall's Eden Project, attracted only a sparse crowd. In London, Kofi Annan, Bill Gates and assorted celebrities urged on the crowd with their own sound bites. People stood for ten hours and those who could not bear to use the lines of chemical toilets urged iron into their bladders.

In Edinburgh, ahead of the G8 summit, 250,000 people dressed in white, the 'Make Poverty History' colour, linked hands and ringed the old city. If those at Hyde Park were mostly young, a good number of those at Edinburgh were older, more sedate citizens – but, to pipe bands rather than electric guitars, they were going to make their own stand. At the concerts and demonstrations around the world people willed the politicians to listen. Old or young, these are the spiritual children of Mandela. When he spoke of justice rather than charity, they all listened. Stand up, be counted, be made to suffer, endure, endure again, endure until the limestone on your prison island burns out your tear ducts, emerge, and still show such grace, pity and compassion that even your enemies are impressed and ashamed. And then, when they are shamed, forgive them. To the apolitical young, or the wearied politicized old, this was morality so above the norm that not one of the world leaders gathering at Edinburgh can stand close and not be dwarfed. Mandela was a most imperfect president, but the young want saints and miracles, not politicians, Geldof is still nicknamed 'Saint' Bob and if Mandela is the father of the crowds, Geldof is the older son, urging on his siblings to try harder at compassionate justice.

The highlight of the concert came in mid-afternoon. It was obvious what was going to happen as soon as the music from The Cars' old record began to be piped through. 'Who's going to take you home tonight?' It had been used in 1984 as the music played over the terrifying images of dying children filmed in Ethiopia by the television reporter, Michael Buerk. When they hit the screens in 1984 the Western world was stunned. It was then that a furious almost-failed musician leapt into action, and Geldof found his vocation. Now, they began playing the images again, and the huge screens in Hyde Park filled with the dying skeletal children. They *know* they are going to die. Their expressions are of despair, and the terrifying nature of Buerk's film is that he moves slowly, lingeringly, but onwards from one to another – to another and another – and the viewers all know the children are going to die. In Hyde Park the film comes to an end, freeze-framing a last emaciated child, teeth bared because she no longer has energy even to shut her mouth. This is Geldof as theatrical impresario now. He is going to pull every heart string going. With a flourish before the completely silent crowd, he introduces a beautiful grown young woman. She is dressed in white Ethiopian robes. Her hair is coiffed and plaited in the extravagant Ethiopian manner. She has just passed her agricultural exams. Her mouth

14

is open in the most dazzling smile. And she is the child of the frozen frame. Somehow she had survived. Geldof claims the credit from the concern and funds raised from his 1984 Live Aid concert and movement. This is of course a ridiculous claim. The film was taken well before Live Aid. But Geldof is saying that the concert goers can make a difference. The young woman is cited as visible evidence. The woman speaks a few words. They are in Amharic or Tigrayan. No one in the audience understands a word. Even her interpreter merely summarizes what she has said. No one can remember the rushed syllables of her very foreign name. (It is in fact Birhan Weldu.) No one cares. She is there as evidence that the crowd will make a difference in the very near future. All a saint needs is a resurrection, and Geldof now validates the huge, entire effort. And, frankly, to organize all that, in so many cities, was an effort. Madonna comes on stage to sing. She too is dressed in white. She hugs the young woman. Then she sings, for once she does not mime, and she does a frankly dynamite set. And, if even the Queen of Pop can be moved, usually so rehearsed and calculated as to be ice cold in her professionalism – but now she is singing with something that is believably passion and, yes, despite all the studio tricks and hundreds of earlier lip-synced concerts, she has a very fine voice – then everybody in the audience is also moved. And they want to move the G8 leaders convening very soon. They want to be the dawn of a new history. They are a noble generation – and they are very naïve.

The summit looms

But Prime Minister Blair is in Singapore, supporting London's bid to host the Olympics. He has missed the concert. It is left to the Chancellor of the Exchequer, Gordon Brown, to answer the interview questions about whether the popular pressure will influence the summit. But Africa and debt relief have always been Brown's projects. He has much at stake over the next few days. He answers always positively, reassuringly. Something is being done. Behind the scenes, like 500 frantic roadies at Geldof's event, his officials scramble for broad presummit agreements with the officials of the USA and France in particular. Only Japan is on-target when it comes to aid; but the Japanese want to control their own giving, what they call their 'sunshine policy', and they need to be made part of a coordinated, multilateral effort. George Bush is angling to trade off increased aid for Africa against having to reduce US energy consumption. Even then, his increases will be modest and conditional. France is doing all in its diplomatic power simply to embarrass Tony Blair for as long as possible, right up to the eve of the summit. And these world leaders might not have been much influenced by the concert anyway. Blair, from time to time, is seen strumming his Fender Stratocaster – the 'correct' guitar for rock stars of his generation; black too, just like Eric Clapton's – except that it is a Stratocaster in the Squier series, the downmarket range. Blair, in trying too hard, fails the hip test. Labels count in the world of guitar gods. Japan's Koizumi, long hair always permed (that's how he gets his cavalier curls), has released albums of his favourite tracks. An acid rock fan, he carries street cred a tad more easily than the hair-transplanted plastic-surgeried Berlusconi of Italy. And George Bush, for all his enjoyment of Bono's company, once thought the Taliban were a rock band. It is not an encouraging line-up for the most important gig of Africa's history.

And the summit is, after all, a G8 summit. As well as the

peaceful pro-Africa demonstrators, harder battalions are massing. The street-fighters of Seattle and Genoa are filtering into sleepy Scotland. Even within their networks, the word is out that this summit should not be disrupted too much. They do not want to undermine the Geldof faction. But they have their own crazies as well, and the crazies are showing signs of going for it. From the first clashes it is clear the Scottish riot police have practised a technique of raising their transparent shields and slamming them forward on an angle. They move forward a step and right the angle. They think they are going to drive crowds back in this manner. Some of the crazies will think this is God's gift to serious protesters: they know how to counter this one; they do their preparatory work on computer simulations, and they go into impact training. And they believe. They are not anarchists. They just do not believe in the governments gathering in Scotland for the summit. They do believe in an end to capitalism.

This is where the essential middle-classness of the Geldof project is revealed. All the young millionaires who played the concert, all the affluent young fans who attended, all of them want to give more because they and their countries have much. More can be spared. How this surplus was accumulated, if the process of accumulation is basically unfair, whether they are the victims of, not a system, but of a *global structure* of ripping off, ripping away from the poorest and turning what has been ripped away into the commodities of a life-style that can be bought, that must be bought, that can only be bought (or stolen), does not cross the minds of those in Hyde Park.

5 July

The very eve: Tony Blair, from Singapore, is spinning that the civil servants from the eight countries have almost got a deal. Jacques Chirac, a late arrival in Singapore, is saying the opposite. He is also saying that British food is awful, and that only Finnish food is worse. The Finns have no votes in the Olympic stakes. There are only the British to wind up. Blair, who arrived early, is leaving. Chirac will leave late. But both men will surely arrive exhausted in Scotland. Either Blair is right, and the deal is almost done – leaving the leaders merely to chat – or Chirac is determined to wreck the deal, or at least make it as difficult as possible. And not just to spite the British, but possibly to forge a new relationship with the Americans – cosy up to Bush on climate change issues – and repair the split over Iraq, while driving at least a temporary wedge between Blair and Bush. Blair is saying a deal is close on climate change – meaning a watered-down agreement with fine words. Some sort of deal is surely on the cards for Africa. But, talking of Iraq, how many multinationals have benefited from its 'reconstruction'? There will be a rush too to 'reconstruct' Africa. In the USA, Britain and France, boardrooms are gearing up. If not a new East India Company or a new British South Africa Company – the corporate means by which colonial Britain exploited India and southern Africa – then a new regime of many Western companies looks poised to ensure the correct, incorruptible delivery of 'aid'. In many ways, the crazies massing in Scotland are correct. All Africa needs now is the readvent of Rhodes many times over.

6 July

Some 5000 protesters march on the Gleneagles site of the summit; 1000 break through the police lines. The spectacle of horse-mounted police and helicopters – old and new technology – drives them back; but, yes, before that, the crazies had smashed past the slamming shields technique like rushing water. The police immediately ban further protests. It is a simple draconian measure: ban what you cannot control; and it is a critique of the police as much as of the protesters.

Only no one cares any more. The news breaks through from Singapore that London has been awarded the Olympic Games. London led Paris in every round and ensured, as each rival city dropped out – Moscow, New York, Madrid – that votes were transferred to London. Simple lobbying did it. The French thought that their style alone would carry the day. In many ways it should have. Paris already had facilities in place. The London Olympics looks good only on paper. But lobbying is a fine art; the French did not do it and now accuse the British of perfidity. The British left no heart string unpulled. Some 30 children of appropriately mixed races were presented to the International Olympic Committee almost as specimens that the games would indeed benefit the young. Futurist video shots of struggling young African athletes, also coming into their prime at London, reinforced the whole Geldof message. There was some pretty arrant piggy-backing, but no one cares about anything anymore but celebration. That evening, miraculously without jet lag (or with very good makeup), Blair and Chirac sit on either side of the Queen for the obligatory black-tie and dinner-jacket photograph. Blair does not do white-tie functions if he can help it; he has no medals to wear. But Chirac is at least gracious in defeat and conspicuously hugs Blair. In the background, not invited to sit for the formal photograph, are the leaders of China, India, Mexico, Brazil and South Africa – the emergings, the understudies for a future G13. Even Kofi Annan has been invited, and he and Vladimir Putin have taken the extraordinary step of inviting African presidents to condemn Robert Mugabe. The Russians, and the Chinese too, see Africa opening up and they have their own corporations. To an extent, Putin's condemnation of Mugabe is also a dig at the Chinese, who already have economic interests in Zimbabwe. It is not only the British who can make the deft and subtly perfidious movement.

7 July

If the Chinese, Indian, Mexican, Brazilian and South African leaders were not invited to sit for the official group portrait they were wheeled out to flank Blair the very next day. Chirac and Bush stood immediately behind him. Bush's eyes kept shifting, but Chirac stared pointedly at Blair's back. A sombre Blair, at his teeth-clenching best, condemned the terrorism that had suddenly struck London – then abruptly left the G8 summit to visit the capital – and that day's talks about climate change were delivered at a stroke to the US position.

In a very clear way, the summit was at that moment hijacked, and all the momentum that Geldof, Gordon Brown and others had sought to generate on behalf of Africa went flat on the very eve of what was meant to have been Africa's day. Even the crazies stopped attacking the venue. Instantly, it was terrorism and the international Islamic insurgency all over again.

What Blair found in London was that typical British example of controlled pandemonium and the typical British determination to understate all things. Everyone knew what the death count was likely to be, but the police stubbornly filtered through the numbers as slowly as possible, leaving long acculturation gaps in between each announcement. Everyone knew what the technique was, but everyone let the police do it.

Everyone was just picking themselves up and refusing to be anything but British. It was one of those legendary phlegmatic days. Only the bombers were probably themselves British. The smart money in the intelligence community is that they were radicalized young British Muslims, and were not part of any al-Qaeda cell, but were a small autonomous action-group well below the chatter-lines upon which the security services eavesdrop. The young bombers just went to King's Cross station during rush hour; they took one bomb on an underground train east, another on one west, a third on one south, and a fourth was carried onto a bus also going south. It is the immediate theory anyway among the shadowy cognoscenti of a strange world. I am offloaded from my train before King's Cross. Something is happening up the line. When I reach my office in Russell Square a huge explosion rings out. It takes several minutes for us to find out that it was the bus. It was literally around the corner, in front of Tavistock Square, where the statue of Ghandi and many memorials against world violence sit. All day sirens blare on the surrounding roads and helicopters dash past my windows. At three o'clock, when the police give an all-clear, hundreds of thousands of Londoners start walking home. Blair flies back to Scotland, swearing the African agenda is not dead.

8 July

It is not dead, but it is not kicking as much as many had hoped. Several African presidents, in addition to South Africa's Mbeki, have been invited for the announcement. Nigeria's Obasanjo is there, so is Ghana's Kuofor, and a handful of others. These are the 'cleans', those inching towards democracy and against corruption. It is very much inching. There are clouds over both Obasanjo and Kuofor, but they are probably the best leaders Nigeria and Ghana are going to get right now. South Africa's Mbeki has just fired his vice-president who is accused of corruption. But one of the members of the Commission for Africa, Ethiopian prime minister Meles Zenawi, is ill-starred right now – having probably foreclosed an election unnecessarily and then come down with a heavy hand on those who complained. His police killed more people than died in the London bombings. Another member of the Commission, Anna Kajumulo Tibaijuka, as the UN's special envoy, is that very day in Zimbabwe lecturing political leaders on their forced removals of township dwellers and the demolition of their homes. Zimbabwe was conspicuous by its almost total absence in the Commission's report. This is one very embarrassing country, and the African presidents do not quite know how to behave towards an embarrassment. Kofi Annan has broken the silence, but he is a UN secretary-general and not a president. Yet even the Commission was prepared to pussy-foot around Robert Mugabe. Almost as if to overshadow him, the little panoply of African leaders is paraded for a photo with the G8 at Gleneagles. The fact that they had clearly made their travel arrangements ahead of time suggests that the deal on Africa had been pretty much agreed before the summit began. All the Geldof effort might just have been window dressing.

Not that Geldof would have known that. He is at pains to vindicate the agreement. He and Bono have also been invited to appear with the African presidents. In front of the cameras Blair makes each G8 president sign the agreement. This has never been done before. This is show business, just as Hyde Park was show business. Japan's Koizumi has grown his luxuriant hair even longer just for the occasion. He could easily have been on stage in the park. And Geldof is edgy and defensive. He is talking like a politician now, essentially saying that big steps have been taken and that this was the best deal available and it will make a big difference. It will, but it is drowned out by his own hype, and the Make Poverty History coalition of pressure groups and non-governmental aid agencies slam into him. The deal is too little, will take too long and Geldof has spent too much time in the company of high men. The angry part of him strutted in Hyde Park and the man of the mahogany tables has turned up at Gleneagles.

What Gleneagles did was to increase G8 aid to $50 billion by 2010. Half of that will go to Africa. In fact, $30 billion of that had been agreed before Gleneagles, and the summit added only another $20 billion – but it is fair to say that Gleneagles consolidated a recent trend. Most of this aid, however, will not come until closer to 2010. Most of it will be programme and project related, which means more money for both Western and African technical consultants, Western agencies and, yes, Western corporations. It can be a merry-go-round. The Japanese have been relaying highways in Zambia. They had only recently been laid with Swedish aid but the Swedish technical consultants had designed the roads for snow conditions.

Gleneagles also agreed to cancel the debt of the 18 poorest African countries. This will be very welcome, but some of these countries have been scrambling to be certified among the poorest; they have no other economic strategy but the anticipation of relief; they have no productive plans or capacity. They will find that the cancellation carries extremely fine print. If funds that would have gone into repayment are now meant to be channelled into education and health then the international monitoring of that diversion will mean a further loss of economic sovereignty. And, of course, the more disparate are the new social projects, the more opportunity there will be to engineer 'leakages', or corruption. Gleneagles did nothing for African trade. African farmers, for instance, will still labour against subsidized American and European agriculturalists. Gleneagles was almost a recipe for increased dependency with no fair means to claw a way out, and a million new means for the dishonest to steal money. And this does not mean only those who are dishonest in Africa.

The spectacle in the reconstruction of Iraq, where a new bridge miraculously costs several times more than any local engineer would estimate it at, suggests that the Western contractor is enjoying the extensive and extended process of reconstruction. The world will come to Africa even more intensely than before. And, when Africa seeks to enter the world, it will be as if to the ecological isolation of the Eden Project in Cornwall, taken seriously by a handful who forsake the spectacle of what the West, in its bounty, might choose to do.

Chapter 2
Corruption

The spectacle of corruption is how we, in the West, see the spectre of corruption with which Africa is ruled. I do not mince my words. There is not a government, democratic or dictatorial, free from it – with perhaps the exception of Eritrea, which is simply free of freedom itself. Outside that monastic enclave there are many governments that cannot function without corruption, and there are governments that exist to be corrupt. That is to put it starkly – although the same stark words could have been said about European, North and South American governments in the nineteenth century and into the twentieth. They remain true for the Indian subcontinent, in Asia, increasingly in China, and certainly in many parts of post-Soviet Europe and the Turkic republics. African corruption has been, however, a spectacle. This is not only because of the ridiculous nature of Emperor Bokassa's coronation – aided and abetted by the French – in what he was able, temporarily, to call the Central African Empire; nor the flaunted kleptomania of Zaire's Mobutu, whose accumulated riches could have repaid the debts of several neighbouring countries; nor in the pervasive footage of rich men and gaudy women in mansions and Mercedes limousines, driving through the slums of those less well off. The spectacle is precisely in the contrast between the mansions and the slums – without even the evidence, available in Brazil and India, that the engines of growth are sufficiently in place to give some, even if tangential, perhaps largely futile, but *some* hope of climbing upwards for those trodden below. The spectacle is that the rich who have plundered live, unconscionably, amid those who will die early deaths amid grinding and implacable poverty; and that the rich are concerned more with their own welfare than the incidental needs of development. But, as with all things, corruption is more complex than the spectacle, no matter how sorry that spectacle is. It might even be a normative condition in many places – something is wrong if there is *no* corruption. I want to explore this complexity. However, I do not wish to deny the aspirations of the young revolutionaries who imagine the invention of the slow-drilling bullet, to be used by the firing squads at the moment of reckoning for those who have stolen hugely and benefited their fellows minutely.

An accounting approach to corruption

I do not want to labour here a certain condition whereby corruption was promulgated by the international policies of the great powers – where aid was given, not for development in the first instance, but to buy political allies. To an alarming extent this still happens in the Middle East, so that US aid has Israel and Egypt as its two largest beneficiaries, precisely to allow the US leverage on both sides of that region's quarrels. Under such conditions, scrutiny of the benefits of African aid – whether it built schools for the poor or palaces for the rulers – was a second-order consideration. I shall return to this theme later in the book.

Here I want to make the further point that, whether governmental corruption involves the ransacking of local resources, or foreign monies, what is at stake here in the relationship with foreign donors or corporations is that there has to be a transaction that involves a foreign capacity to *process* the key ingredients involved in corruption. Thus, war diamonds, whether illegally sold by government figures or warlord factions, must be factory-cut and polished, sorted into quality grades, and ingeniously declared 'clean' for the Amsterdam or other international markets. Thus, if a foreign contractor is awarded development funds to build a bridge or a telecommunications system, the potential 'leakage' of funds will be built into the deliberate over specification of highly technical aspects of the project. A web of subcontracts with companies registered in far-flung havens will progressively launder the leaked funds until they are untraceable. There is a certain *technology* of corruption that involves international cooperation far beyond the shores of Africa.

I wish to make a preliminary distinction, which is also a crude one, but the effects of the distinction can be very visible in voting patterns in African elections – where 'corrupt' candidates receive genuinely popular support. The distinction resides not in the quality of corruption, but in the direction of its 'reinvestment'. Thus, if ransacked funds are deposited in a Swiss account and are drawn upon only to build chalets and mansions in Europe, no one has benefited except the thief and his or her family. If, however, they are used to establish new businesses back home, for instance a bus company, then many people will benefit from employment and transport. The thief may have to be content with a local mansion, built from his or her business profits, but may have garnered a better reputation than the colleague with a Swiss account. It is a crude distinction but, sometimes, the bureaucratic requirements of aid disbursal can be such that it is frankly quicker to release funds in an informal manner.

Finally, and again I shall return to this, there may often be a cultural demand that a leading political and community figure should also be rich. This is both to complete the image required of a senior personage and to facilitate his or her meeting the demands for patronage. The networks of patronage often supersede and, again, may be more efficient than bureaucratic methods for the circulation of funds. It can have, of course, certain democratic drawbacks if people vote only for their benefactor.

There is an addendum from a past time. During the years of apartheid, from the mid-1970s well into the 1980s, various personalities grew very rich in Zambia. This was from the shipment of drugs to South Africa. The recreational drug of choice in Johannesburg night clubs was Mandrax – a barbiturate, a 'downer' or 'spacer' (well, they did use to say 'spaced-out, man' in those days); 50,000 tablets, each selling for five Rand, could fit into a single suitcase. The Mandrax was made in India, flown to Zambia, then driven south to Johannesburg. Even after paying the Indian manufacturer, the freight charges of Zambian Airways (which then had a direct flight to Bombay), bribes for Zambian customs and for transporting the drugs by car to South Africa, a year of such shipments could make the Mandrax tsar a millionaire. The tsars were often government ministers, reducing their costs (and thus swelling their profits) by using government facilities. Their start-up costs probably came from government coffers as well. But they were perceived in Zambia as somewhat heroic crooks. It was one of the few means by which a beleaguered Zambia, deliber-

28

ately destabilized by South Africa, could fight back. There is no longer an apartheid government, and Mandrax has faded into chemical antiquity. The point here is that corruption wears many faces.

This is why, in the midst of many faces, and many different political, moral and cultural considerations, the Commission for Africa's approach to the eradication of corruption is one-dimensional. It starts from twin assumptions. The first is that greater accountancy will reduce 'leakage'. The second is that greater transparency will contribute to greater democracy. To be fair to the Commission, it does recognize faults within both the donor and the recipient communities. However, it is lazy with its diagnosis. It seems true to say that 'corruption is a by-product of weak governance' (Chapter 4.5 para. 88) but the report immediately goes on to criticize weak government procedures within the donor countries. What the report does not point out is that corruption is a by-product of often incredibly sophisticated manipulation of detailed government accounts by government figures. In this case there is 'weak governance' from a form of strong government. This is particularly true in the area of procurement, the buying in of goods and services, which the report rightly identifies as a primary location of corruption. But the report acknowledges that 'politicians, public officials ... bankers, lawyers, accountants, and the engineers working on public contracts' (4.4.1 para. 90) can all be involved – to which it should more explicitly add (but does not) on 'both sides of the transaction'. It is not that the procurement policies and methodologies do not conform to 'best practice'; it is that best practice can be used against its original aim. The creativity of accounting in certain giant US corporations in recent years, with massive financial hardship only upon discovery, suggests how well-developed and manipulable accounting best practice can be – and probably continues to be in corporations where the risk of malpractice has been successfully taken. The answer is not necessarily more scrutiny – that does not in itself lead to better governance – but less export of goods and services. Local capacity building might well be the greatest goal of aid and investment – but that would reduce the profits of corporations outside Africa. This suggestion is of course naïve and to an extent gratuitous. Capacity does not come overnight. But the recommendations of the report are themselves gratuitous. The call for greater independent bodies of scrutiny does not interrogate itself in terms of how and with what priority greater independent scrutiny might be applied in a host of African conditions: corruption certainly, in judicial decisions, in the competitive environment for every educational, medical and social resource; in 53 countries.

The report starts treading dangerous grounds where, in its desperation to suggest measures against corruption, it advocates confiscation of stolen goods *without* the burden of criminal proof (4.5.3 para. 104), thus suggesting stronger measures against corruption by applying weaker standards of law. It is a problem of the report that, in arguably the most important aspect of its deliberations, it has come up with the weakest conclusions. I wish to add a critique of the cultural assumptions of the report in the section that follows. Greater transparency will not automatically lead to greater democracy if it disrupts what are now often beneficial systems of patronage. It can instead lead to exactly the sort of destabilization of government that stamping down on interest groups can generate in the West – except that in Africa the interest groups have a composition and social dynamic pretty much ignored throughout the report.

Little fellows need the big man

There is an assumption that African corruption starts at the top, and that the remedy must be the ability to change the top. The problem is that corruption has not radically diminished, but in some cases grown, in the democratically changed governments of most African countries. It might be brought more under control, in other words it is reined in where it disrupts the capacity of government to be government; the government might be corrupt, but it needs to be a government – otherwise it cannot be corrupt. It can eat the nation; to an extent it can eat the state; but, beyond a certain point, the government cannot eat itself. The 'big men' who fall are those who have over-stepped this mark.

But the top is corrupt precisely because it is a bifurcated top. One part of it is a formalized government charged with the entire nation's welfare; the other part is an informalized welfare system in which patronage rewards the loyalty of support groups and interest groups that may be ethnic or familial, but which is both a variation of the 'old school tie' syndrome in England (albeit a gross variation), and a continuation of social systems that allowed African subjects to circumvent the formal demands of colonialism. There is no change now because the systems of patronage are entrenched and, in very poor countries, what are now 'citizens' as opposed to 'subjects', must nevertheless subject themselves to the 'big men' in order to secure some benefit of development or even survival. The remedy for corruption must involve both the ability to change the top and the ability to change the social system, with the latter guaranteeing some means of support for those at the bottom. The combination of democracy and liberal economics does not do this.

Moreover, the whole concept of the 'big man' is not an exclusively African phenomenon. The expression 'liege Lord' is not long dead in Britain, and its connotation of power and economic control is what is at stake in Africa. The 'big man' must be economically viable in order to be seen as in control. Side by side with modern systems of formal government are variations of 'feudal' governance – albeit without the compulsory hereditary requirements – and this form of governance is not weak at all. The Commission for Africa is plainly misconceiving the issue. On this side of the coin, governance is very strong.

V. S. Naipaul's famous *A Bend in the River* tracks a journey into what was Zaire. In a section called 'The Big Man' he describes the omnipresence of portraits of the president. What is at stake here, as Naipaul tellingly and bitterly infers, is that the pervasiveness of the portrait reflects the pervasiveness of corruption. Seen in Naipaul's terms only the combination of power and corruption is directed downwards, and all claims to development as a goal or benefit in itself are fraudulent. This is the syndrome Crawford Young calls *Bula Matari*, 'he who crushes rocks'. In Naipaul's rendition, corruption cannot be fought unless the power that accompanies it is also fought, but this power can crush its challengers. The way Crawford Young relates it, *Bula Matari* was a term first coined to describe Henry Stanley's blasting his way through the rocky rapids of the Congo River – and there is a tendency to locate today's African social ills in a colonial origin. Patrick Chabal speaks for a generation of Africanists who argue that the postcolonial state could not have a benign or beneficial effect because its origin was not organic. He says that the African state is both 'over-developed and soft'. It is overdeveloped because it was fastidiously and artificially put into place. All the textbook institutions of a state and its government are present. It is soft because, although powerful, it cannot *administer* welfare. Such administration of welfare as does take place tends instead to occur through the informal systems of patronage that bind interest groups to rulers or factions of the ruling elite. This observation gave rise to the controversial work that Chabal later penned with Jean-Pascal Daloz, *Africa Works*, which makes the claim that, after all, there might be a way of perceiving Africa as quite efficient – if only one were to remove Western lenses.

There are three quite powerful ameliorations of this view. The first, by Jean-François Bayart, is a compassionate analysis. It talks of a 'yoke paradigm' which is twofold. The Western world imposes its own yoke, but there is also a local yoke that is imposed by both a merciless nature and a dull tradition. However, Christopher Clapham takes issue with this. Any view of the African state, Clapham argues, must be characterized by the poverty of its material base. It is not a 'dull tradition' but an active and historical one, where African political tradition sees power as a means of controlling economic resources. Having said that, the present state is not an idealizable modernization of what went before, but is constantly undergoing its own institutional changes. Africa is not doomed to remain as a contemporary variant of what went before.

Conservative US political scientists are more emphatic. William Zartman states bluntly that authoritarianism and tyranny are to blame for African state malfunction. And it must be said that much public opinion of Africa is still coloured by the view articulated in 1968 by Aristotle Zolberg who, in a defining article, talked of failure, coercion and conflict. If ever any academic article reinforced the popular (and selective) image of Conrad's *Heart of Darkness*, this was it. But it means, for our purposes, that no talk of corruption can be conducted without intimate intertwining with talk about power. When Mwai Kibaki won the 2002 Kenyan elections, these were hailed in the West as a democratic breakthrough – after the years of authoritarian rule under Daniel Arap Moi. But his followers were heard to whisper, 'now it is our turn to eat'.

Many bends in many rivers

As noted above, it is when too much is eaten by too few, with too little discernibly entering the patronage system, and too few at the bottom benefiting, that popular outrage begins. That outrage may lead nowhere because, after all, it must confront those who are not only greedy but are also powerful. A state may be 'overdeveloped' in the sense of maintaining (and patronizing) a coercive security system; but it may also be 'soft' if that patronage does not reach the junior officers and subalterns. An entire second generation of African coups came not from generals, or even colonels, but from captains and even non-commissioned officers. I speak of military coups later but, for now, I want to make two points. The first is that, in a situation of very scarce resources, pluralism – whether expressed via political parties or other means – is a contest for control of those resources, and control over the retention and *distribution* of those resources. They will be retained by the 'big men' of whatever wins the pluralist struggle, and distributed (in part) to their followers. Again, I shall say more about pluralism later.

The second point is that those outside the developed state will not necessarily rest content, but find ingenious acts of everyday resistance. In the 1980s, when my Ghanaian friend intecepted the passage of a stolen car in Zambia, he knew it had been stolen in South Africa; it was being driven through Zambia, and was destined to be driven through Zaire, finally to be sold in Senegal or some other part of the Francophonie. My friend, who was living in Zambia, simply saved them the trouble of further driving and bribing of customs officials. But he had stumbled upon an amazing multinational cast of car thieves – more accurately, a car thieving syndicate. Senegalese, Zaireans, Zambians and Zimbabweans were all involved, not to mention non-white South Africans: if the elite drove Mercedes Benzs bought with stolen money, the next level down drove Peugeot 504s that had simply been stolen outright. This is a caricature of an uneven and complex situation, but the idea of levels of engagement with informality is real enough. In the slums of Addis Ababa it is a rewarding spectacle – if your honestly gained car breaks down – to walk down the street of Somali mechanics who have produced quite good working replicas of every mechanical part a car owner might need. What I am saying here is that, at the highest levels, informality involves a ransacking of government projects. It is the public sector that is ransacked because the private sector is not developed enough for the sorts of corporate corruption we see in the West. The real effort at a private sector, unfinanced by any World Bank funds for a liberal economy, takes place amid a very different informality to that which facilitates the 'privatization' of large public funds higher up. But it is not a process that is accountable, transparent, or reliably peaceful. Indeed, the small-scale informal sector can be violent and criminal. It is, however, much more complex than the mere sight of street vendors would suggest – and it is without frontiers. It works in cities, so that those who miss out are peasants, particularly pastoralists dependent on rains for their wandering herds. Even in the cities, it is not pretty. The advent of a 'Latin American *barrio* culture', where electricity is hot-wired, and resistance is constant whisper, is also the consolidation of a lawlessness, a state-softness in key motors of the nation. There are different sorts of criminality therefore: that of the 'big man' and those of the ingenious poor. The latter reads more romantically, but is barely a mask for poverty all the same.

Even so, what is required is some way to facilitate the growth and development of the informal sector so that its enterprises become medium-level formal sector players – occupying the underpopulated niche between state and privatized (former state) corporations, and urban subsistence operations. The present situation, however, is where the true 'double yoke' is apparent. The international financial agencies will not bank on what is informal, that is unaccountable; governments seek to licence, regulate, bureaucratize and control rather than facilitate. Regulation is over-developed, but the concern for actual proliferation of economic growth points is soft.

Left where it is, the informal sector remains a site of permeability, namely it can be ransacked by law and order; but it is also a site of resistance, in other words it always springs up again defiantly – and necessitously, since the formal sector in most African countries is not growing. It is in the informal sector that barbed humour grows. In Zambia, the Mandrax tsars drove BMWs as their ostentation of choice. One tsar's name began with 'W', so the acronym became 'Buy Mandrax from W'.

It is this sort of humour that becomes institutionalized in the formal vehicles of free expression that have indeed grown up with democratization. The political cartoon is as developed in its characterization and satire as anything Gilray devised. And political satire, when its writers are not persecuted, can be as biting as anything in the West. Roy Clarke may be of English origin, but 42 years of residence in Zambia saw a fusion between his Yorkshire humour and that of his adopted neighbours. His lampooning of former President Chiluba, known in Clarke's columns as 'Kafupi', sees the diminutive politician as a cross-dressing Imelda Marcos figure, forever buying high-heeled shoes in a fruitless attempt to appear taller – and successfully 2.5 inches more ridiculous. The unconcealed rider to Kafupi's vanity is that he was also a thief, and the shoes were the least of what he had stolen. When Chiluba's successor, Mwanawasa, sought to deport Clarke (for having compared the elephantine Mwanawasa with an elephant), Clarke's editor leapt to his defence; and did so again in the preface to Clarke's collected columns. Fred M'membe wrote that, after all, Clarke was merely continuing a noble African tradition of ribaldry, where even Shaka Zulu could be ritualistically made fun of, to his face, at his own court. Robert Pelton, in his anthropological study of what he called the African 'trickster', subtitled his work *A Study of Mythic Irony and Sacred Delight*. Irony and delight in criticism, at least, are apparent in the regard in which the corrupt are held. There may be no choice but to abide the 'big men' and their ways, there may be little choice but to seek out their patronage, but that does not mean that people like it or will refrain from ridicule. The burgeoning African music industry, with protest lyrics from Nigeria's Fela to Zimbabwe's Mutukudzi, is further evidence of anger against the powerful and corrupt. This is articulated at greater length in the novels of Africa.

On the penultimate page of Ngugi wa Thiongo's anthemic novel, *Petals of Blood*, there is probably the most scathing – and succinct – rendition in African literature of what popular resistance is against: 'Imperialism: capitalism: landlords: earthworms. A system that bred hordes of round-bellied jiggers and bedbugs with parasitism and cannibalism as the highest goal in society.' But it is in the earlier Ghanaian novel, *The Beautyful Ones are Not Yet Born*, by Ayi Kwei Armah, that the luminous nature of a man alone, refusing to be corrupt – even though living and working in literal scatological conditions – shines through. It is almost metaphysical in its aspiration, with the novel's final image of 'a single flower, solitary, unexplainable, very beautiful'. This is the true spectacle of African corruption – although some might say Armah has depicted it almost as a passion play – that the Unbeautyful Ones will one day enter physical and moral collapse and be swept into history; but, in the meantime, they make their excremental extrusion onto the African stage.

Chapter 3
Ethnicity

The connotations of African 'tribalism' are explicit in the Western imagination. It connotes a primitive era, pre-nationalist, premodern, divisive and opening easily onto violence and slaughter – in the case of Rwanda, onto genocide. It is a word less immediately associated with recent history in the Balkans; in Iraq, where ethnicity is a factor, the vocabulary is of ethnicity and clans; in other parts of the world the term 'separatist struggle' covers a multitude of schisms that would, in Africa, be 'tribal' as much as anything else; and where the word is used, as with the North American Indians, 'tribe' has come to denote something residually noble – in Canada, tribes have been subsumed into a politically-correct and revisionist term, and all tribes are now jointly the First Nation – nothing prenationalist here.

Particularly since the 1980s, the entire anthropological literature on 'tribalism', on ethnicity, has seen major shifts. It is fair to say there are competing paradigms, and some of these have enabled major revisionisms of African history. It is now possible to say that there were seldom such entities as African 'tribes', except that they were the creations of colonial administration – of an accounting and transparent administrative system – which needed to define, categorize and then administer people, often balancing the interests and benefits gained from one group against another; what used to be more plainly described as 'divide and rule'.

It is probably true that such revisionism has overstated the case. There could not have been so many language groups in Africa, for instance, if they did not also reflect many different forms of social and political organization. It is not that there were great pluralisms, divisions, shifting alliances, migrations, conquests, assimilations and federalisms – each of these very different dynamisms occurred – but what it was that each achieved group *stood for*, or was made to stand for. The social process of standing for something, an identity, a form of self-understanding, is complex. It may have voluntary and forced elements; and new traditions can become 'old' very quickly, particularly in oral histories where time-cycles can be collapsed into very short generations, but it is almost certainly the case that something primordial exists in most African ethnic groupings. It is also the case that modernization, global and continental influences, the melting pots of cities, metropolitan languages such as English, French and Portuguese – not to mention relatively new religions such as Christianity and Islam before it – have profoundly altered the primordial base. Even more profoundly, the processes of resistance, assimilation, syncretic adaptations of what is new, fusing it in altered shapes onto what was 'old', have led to 'ethnicities' that are dynamic enough also to be polyglot. It is a brave person who simply says that the colonialists achieved today's ethnic map by dividing and ruling.

The report of the Commission for Africa is astoundingly coy about tribalism and ethnicity. Where it is, briefly, mentioned at all, it is quickly skirted. More particularly, blame is skirted – as in the case of Rwanda. The report attributes the ethnic divi-

40

sions in Rwanda solely to colonial divide-and-rule policies. 'This created both artificial divisions and new hierarchies within groups and sowed seeds for conflicts after the colonial leaders departed' (Chapter 3.4.1 para. 23). Almost incorrigibly, Western agencies never learnt not to do this. 'In pre-genocide Rwanda, development assistance reinforced ethnic tension' (Chapter 5.2.1 para. 29). There is not much else by way of analysis in the report, so that the Rwandans themselves, Hutu and Tutsi, are left blameless – but in that case there would be no need for the subsequent tribunals to hear crimes against humanity. Just as war criminals cannot claim they were only part of a preconditioned machine, so too there is a need to accept that African agency can often premeditate and commit atrocity. There may be colonial roots to conflict, but those are not the only ones.

Rwanda

The tenth anniversary of the 1994 slaughters in Rwanda brought Hollywood to the commemoration. *Hotel Rwanda* touched those who knew little about what had happened, and injected a heroism into a strangely muted tragedy – muted because of concerns for audience ratings. The truly horrific killings were underplayed and the news footage (again, not all of it broadcast) on which some scenes were based tells a some-what stronger story. Peter Raymont's 2005 release, *Shake Hands with the Devil*, traces the return to Rwanda of Romeo Dallaire, the Canadian officer who commanded the UN blue berets who, under-staffed and under-mandated, did not pre-vent the killings and, militarily, did not even try. For Dallaire, the true heart of darkness was not in Rwanda itself, but the heartless bureaucracy of the UN – not a faceless bureaucracy, for Kofi Annan as Deputy Secretary-General bore a visible responsibility. There are times when caution, procedure and even-handedness are not the hallmarks of a statesman. For Dallaire, who must also bear some responsibility – he asks whether, as the ranking field officer, he should have resigned in protest – the Western indifference was as great a crime as the Hutu slaughter of the Tutsis. It was not just indifference, however. Gerard Prunier has written compellingly of a calculated French refusal to deploy their own peacekeeping forces to prevent what happened. They stood aside on a whim of the Quai D'Orsay that a Hutu government would remain more committed to the Francophonie, and thus to France, and that there had been disturbing traces of Anglophilia among the Tutsi leadership.

The standing-aside was a significant action in itself – because it was not a refusal to engage with mob action. It was a refusal to engage with formal institutions gearing up for brutality. As Timothy Longman has pointed out, the genocide of the Tutsis and moderate Hutus took meticulous planning by government and military officials. This was evidence of excessively strong government – nothing weak here – determined to cleanse the nation, to deny a huge part of the population the right to membership of the nation. It was also, as Longman intimates, a clash between the coercive capacity of the state and the rising activisms of civil society. What was at stake here was a mixture of primordialisms, colonial exacerbations of them, international politics – both of indifference and cynicism – meticulous government planning and coercive capacity, and a contest between open society and top–down authoritarianism. The cocktail was much more than pure rival ethnicities, and with many more mixes than a single colonial intervention. The problem with so many analyses is their reductionism, the search for a clean answer. The fractions of an answer are murky and ambiguous.

Some distinctions

What follow are fractions of an answer as much as distinctions. However, it is fair to say that the scholarly thought on ethnicity contains five strands. The first is very much that ethnicity is a device deliberately used by politicians, even exaggerated by them. This was once to emphasize a difference from the outside world, to be able to respond to Western pressure for democracy by maintaining that African countries were too divided and not yet ready for it. More parochially, it can be used by politicians within a country to build up a power base.

Secondly, drawing from the major current paradigm in social anthropology, it is said that ethnicity has been 'imagined' into place. It is a social construct – an act of imagination and will. This is not to say, however, that imagination assumes a dynamic of its own. What might earlier have been imagined may be developed, even reconstructed, by politicians – who are successful in this because no overarching civil society has yet been achieved within the state. In short, imagination and the reinforcement of imagination are successful in the absence of rival identities.

However, thirdly, in conditions of scarce resources, it might be very difficult to find satisfactory other identities – particularly away from cities with their associational possibilities. The search for resources can take place best in groups of great cohesion, even if that cohesion is narrowly and exclusively defined. A 'tribe' can have its own internal 'civil society' and, in any case, it can aspire to play its own role in the wider civil society of the state. In this latter sense there might not be a better-organized pressure group for most of its members. Ethnicity in short can have a very real material base.

Having said that, almost every African country fought for its independence as a nation, and not as a tribe or ethnic group. The independence struggle created its own social discourse and social and political *mythos* into which all bought. It was its own new imagination. So, fourthly, there is no ethnic identity and loyalty that is not at least rivalled by a national one. In this view people may have multiple identities and lead complex lives of choice and balancing.

Finally, precisely because of independence, there is an international *de jure* identity of the state into which all ethnic groups are subsumed. In international law the state has its own legal personality. Internally, it has its own legal instruments and constitutional care of itself. Against this, any political usage of ethnicity must be *plotted*, as indeed it was in Rwanda. To this extent, even if there were primordial elements in the racism that erupted there, they were not spontaneous primordial acts.

The gestating nation

If some say that tribalism was the result of colonialism, the modern concept of the nation certainly was. The 53 states of Africa, embodying 53 'nations', had never existed before nor, a mere 100 years before independence, been conceived of before, either by those whose continent it was, or those who were about to colonize it. In the event, that nationalism has been as successful as it has been is miraculous, and is a sign of an immense step into modernity for the whole continent.

It was not an easy step. The fault lines of artificial, composite states showed through quickly. The colonial powers granted state independence. It was left to their new governments to sustain – in many cases, create – nations. The interesting thing is how unoriginal some of these steps of creation were. And even in cases where the new state was endangered by break-aways, those very breakaways sought to follow exactly the same steps. At the end of the 1960s there was the spectacle of the army of Biafra, a secessionist 'state' from Nigeria, marching off to war to the music of the new national anthem – drawn from Sibelius's *Finlandia Suite*. The point here is how recent Finnish nationalism then was – less than a half century earlier – and how important Sibelius had been to what the (newly reconstructed) 'old' epic poem called 'the nation growing'. If the artefacts of attempted-nationalism were not novel, the reconciliation that followed Biafra's defeat and reabsorption back into Nigeria was a testament to what a combination of nationalism and humaneness can do – although it should also be said that the wartime suffering of the Biafran civilian popu-lation was anything but humane. In 1968, as a young student, the Biafran cause was the very first that attracted my political and fund-raising involvement. International volunteer pilots flew relief shipments. A small number of states, including Czechoslovakia and Zambia, gave Biafra diplomatic recog-nition. The Biafrans had good public relations but also, back then, it was not assumed that the states of African indepen-dence had to remain just as they were. Ghana's Kwame Nkrumah had been calling for a federation, a United States of Africa, and everything was simultaneously anxious to be 'national' and in flux. The crisis and bloodshed in Congo had been the worst of all.

In 1961 when the UN Secretary-General, Dag Hammarskjöld,

was mysteriously killed in an attempt to resolve the Congo crisis it was widely thought that both his death and that of the first Congolese prime minister, Patrice Lumumba, had been assassinations orchestrated from different ends of the cold war. Hammarskjöld's plane blew up over the Zambian town of Ndola, just south of the Congo border. When Zambia became independent in 1964 one of its early acts was to build a memorial to Hammarskjöld. Near Ndola sits a shrine, and it is planted for a mile around in Swedish pine. It remains a most plangent symbol – but it also memorializes the fact that, with the new African nationalisms, came an international politics that was not benign.

Zambia inherited the problems of both. A year after its independence, in 1965, the neighbouring country of Rhodesia made its Unilateral Declaration of Independence. This was a desperate attempt on the part of white settlers to preserve their minority rule. It was likened at the time by Whitehall mandarins to a situation where only the inhabitants of Brighton could be rulers of Britain. The weakness of the British government, under Harold Wilson, meant that the settlers – for 15 years – got away with it. In the meantime, the superpowers weighed into the continent's struggles, and supported the apartheid regime in South Africa. Zambia, cut off from the sea and wanting to observe UN sanctions against Rhodesia, had its economic potential compromised at the outset. With more than 80 language groups within its borders it also had a problem with establishing a lasting sense of nationalism. Although much maligned, even ridiculed, towards the end of his time, the Zambian President Kaunda's tripartite efforts to foster unity – judicious regional representation in every sphere of government, a national philosophy of his own creation called 'humanism', and a one-party state – worked. These were coupled with what was essentially a propaganda campaign. Every television and radio programme was interspersed with the slogan 'One Zambia, One Nation', and the national anthem laboured the line 'all one, proud and free', and thanked God for the privilege. And that was probably Kaunda's fourth weapon, a religiosity that made much of forgiveness, reconciliation, pacificism, and their endowment by God's grace. Against such an armoury, any prospective secessionists shied away – or were crushed in a thinly concealed and very political, not Christian, ruthlessness. It is interesting that, in the South Africa of the 1990s, many of these instruments were again visible – including the religiosity. Without Desmond Tutu there might not have been such a successful Nelson Mandela. The task of nation-building must use no doubt sincere artifice. Tutu and Kaunda were the showmen of God.

But the project of nationalism is far from complete in Africa. Just two years after the successful advent of black majority rule in Rhodesia, and its rebirth as Zimbabwe, the atrocities and pogroms that began in 1982 and stretched to 1987 wreaked havoc in the western provinces of Matabeleland North and South. There was an ethnic component and a political rivalry, but it was Ndebele casualties at the hands of a Shona army unit – the North Korean-trained Fifth Brigade – that bore sorry witness to ethnic tensions in what was meant to have been a glorious new nation. The long-running civil war in Angola was fought on issues of political rivalry, control of economic resources, and ethnic strongholds – egged on and supported for years by cynical international powers. There continues to be fractiousness in Uganda, and great tensions in Sudan –

following the death of the southern leader, John Garang. In these two last cases, religion and ethnicity intermingle as animating causes of conflict. But, in all the conflicts cited in this paragraph, every one has some mixture of causes, of which ethnicity is one. But it means that the problem of nationalism in Africa is not reducible to a case simply of tribe vs nation.

None of this even begins to discuss the perhaps larger issues of poverty and wealth distribution. There is certainly an emerging class structure in Africa, but lack of an industrialized working class (because of a lack of industrialization), a huge *lumpenproletariat* in the urban informal sector, a larger peasant population in the countryside, the fact that religions may be not only the 'opium of the masses' but dynamic sites of resistance, and the question of ethnicity all make the debate on class formation a vexed one. Describing the elite as *compradors*, as collaborators with Western capital, is made problematic in that so often the elite, far from being masters of local accumulation by ransacking national resources and passing these onto the global world of capitalism, ransack international resources that enter their country as aid.

Whatever the debate, something that stratifies, that separates and confines is occurring. Even in the newly-liberated Eritrea of 1993, official idealism permeating the air, I could not take a walk down the main street of Asmara without being confronted by young boys and teenagers – not begging, for beggars had been rather roughly swept from the streets – wanting to talk to the exotic visitor. Then, I had very long hair and, referring to the ubiquitous kung fu films, the boys would say, 'only the masters can wear hair like that,' to which I would reply naively, 'you are your own masters now.' The boys would take my hands, approve of the calluses on my knuckles, but notice callus-free palms, then show me their own. 'Do you think that what has been won has been won for us? We shall remain poor. Only the masters can hope like you.' Their knowing smiles would chasten me. These days I defend asylum seekers from Eritrea before the UK immigration tribunals. Poor boys drafted into the army to fight the war against Ethiopia that their masters did not need to wage. There has not been a single conflict to which the independent state of Eritrea has rushed to fight that could not have been settled by negotiation. Being left to poverty is one form of disregard, being used as cannon-fodder is a step further. But the border war with Ethiopia was also in the name of nationalism.

Despite many threats and attempts – Biafra being a case in point – there have only been two secessions from the boundaries bequeathed by colonialism: Congo Brazzaville from Congo or Zaire, and Eritrea from Ethiopia. There is an effort at the present time on the part of Somalia to secede from Somaliland, but that is not gaining any international support or recognition; and the secessionist efforts in western and southern Sudan have had a chequered and unsuccessful history. There has been, by contrast, a successful amalgamation of Tanganyika and Zanzibar to form Tanazania. All in all the project of nationalism has stuck reasonably well. Perhaps it is because there is no real alternative. African states have enough trouble surviving as they are. Fragmentation would generally not help economic progress. And the processes of 'continentalization' and globalization have had positive impacts on nationalism. The Africa Cup of Nations, the continental football trophy, attracts passionate support for national teams; there is probably no greater delight than the Olympic Games and the spectacle of Ethiopian and Kenyan distance-runners and Nigerian sprinters thrashing all comers. And globalization makes cultural inroads as well. The sight of Jamaican-influenced Rastas and New York-influenced ghetto fashions and rap are cases in point. New identities are being formed and added to the old. They may not immediately supplant the old, but they provide more complex choices and mixes.

What is the 'tribal' part of identity has often been itself the product of mixtures. Shaka Zulu's conquests meant the growth of a Zulu nation and the incorporation of many into a new identity. Some who escaped Shaka took refuge in the mountains and became the Sesotho people of what is now Lesotho. And the wandering offshoots of Shaka's empire set up homes in what is now Zimbabwe as the Ndebele people, in Zambia as the Ngoni, and added new characteristics to their culture and identity.

The older characteristics sometimes die hard. In the simmering civil violence that pervaded KwaZulu after majority rule finally came to South Africa, Zulu attackers would set upon 'opposition' ANC villages with the 'bull-horn' enveloping tactics used by Shaka – attacking in a pincer movement (the horns), with the looters, usually women, then coming in as the cradle of the horns. But South Africa itself provides the shining example of what a rainbow nation actually means. It does not come without great difficulties and reluctances, but it means a fought-for and eventually thoughtful unity irrespective of race and that means irrespective of 'tribal' ethnicities.

All the traditional 'tribal' affiliations can be subsumed under a political momentum for change. The political successors to Kaunda disappointed their followers in Zambia, but the popular will to replace him swept all corners of the nation. At any compass point in the electoral campaign of 1991, the two-fingered gesture that was adopted to indicate that Kaunda's time was up became a brief national emblem.

None of this is to deny the continued existence of 'tribal' identities and their often baleful influences. The slaughters of Rwanda are a scar that cannot be explained away as someone else's fault. Africa can do without the patronization that infers there is no blame except far away. There can still be something rotten in the heart of Africa, but it is not anything simple. Because it is complex and dynamic it can partake in something very positive. At the end of a half-century of independence the national borders are now sealed into the future; the nationalism within them is perhaps, in most cases, also gelling. It has been a most compelling and compressed process. It is not often that 53 nations are established and are expected to succeed in one generation.

Chapter 4
Dictatorship and democracy

T he still-abiding image of the African dictator may or may not be racist. After all, there is still an abiding image of the South American dictator – usually a military general with gold epaulets and a thin moustache, oily and sinister. The African variant is more buffoonish: Idi Amin brought something to a view of Africa that has not yet been erased. But there have been many types of African dictatorship and many levels of 'democracy' in more recent times, not to mention efforts to dictate exactly what democracy should deliver. Robert Mugabe would have won the 2005 parliamentary elections without rigging, but he wanted not just a victory but a nationwide validation that allowed him dictatorship by 'democratic' means. Mugabe has become the potential successor figure to Amin, and he represents a complexity never associated with Amin. Highly educated, with five degrees, able to speak English more faultlessly than most of his white critics, and with a record as a volatile unpredictable chameleon, he fits no stereotype. In Africa today there is no stereotype of dictatorship, and none of democracy either. A rough typology would probably look like this:

Dictatorship

1. Ruthless, military-originated, family-based kleptomania: Mobutu of Zaire.
2. Ridiculous-seeming military splendour: Amin of Uganda and Jean-Bédel Bokassa of the briefly-named Central African Empire.
3. Ruthless military dictatorship, crudely reliant on cultural manipulation as much as force of arms: Taylor of Liberia.
4. Ruthless military dictatorship with, all the same, a technocratic base: Abacha of Nigeria.
5. Technocratic military dictatorship with impulses towards the return of civilian democracy: Obasanjo of Nigeria in the 1970s.
6. Idealistic military dictatorship involving younger officers: Rawlings of Ghana and Sankara of Burkina Faso.
7. Incompetent military dictatorship involving younger officers: Momoh of Sierra Leone.

The 'dictatorship' of the one-party state

8. Patronizing elder statesman-led one-party states: Kaunda's Zambia, Nyerere's Tanzania.
9. Self-aggrandizing presidential one-party states: Banda's Malawi.

Low-intensity democracy

10. The dominant-party state, where opposition is allowed but ruthlessly kept within careful limits: Mugabe's Zimbabwe.
11. Pluralist states where the parties mirror ethnic groupings: Rwanda.
12. States that hold 'democratic' elections but amid corruption

and decentralized rigging: Mwanawasa's Zambia, Obasanjo's current Nigeria.

Actually democratic states

13. Probably as close as there are to such states in Africa
today, none without problems: South Africa, Botswana
(but see below), Ghana, some would say to an extent
Kenya and Mozambique.

The typology is not exclusive, and many other examples could
have been used in most categories. The typology is, however,
indicative. Government is not easily defined in Africa. More
over, it has to be said that many dictators and one-party states
enjoyed, at least for a time, extensive popular support. This
can certainly be said for the early regimes of Kaunda, Nyerere,
Rawlings and Sankara. It has also to be said that, on occasion,
military dictatorships were able to establish the preconditions
for more democratic successors – preconditions that democratic governments could not easily have achieved. The military government of Obasanjo created a more multifaceted
sense of pluralism in Nigeria, so that 'democracy' was no
longer a crude balancing act among a very small number of
large regional blocs.

And there is an important *caveat* here, one usually over-
looked by Western political pressure: even if a state holds free
and fair elections, there is no guarantee that elections alone
guarantee the free and fair treatment of citizens and residents.
Botswana, for instance, is ostensibly democratic in its electoral
processes. It does not always guarantee the right to free
expression. The story in 2005 of Professor Ken Good is a case
in point.

The saga of Ken Good

Ken Good was my colleague at the University of Zambia in the early 1980s. He was, even then, a meticulous and careful political scientist, not given to blowing his own trumpet, and hardly a public activist. Instead, he was, in his academic papers, reasoned and critical. He was certainly critical of the government of Kenneth Kaunda, but always on the basis of carefully footnoted evidence. Indeed, in the days before electronic archives, Ken's huge, annotated and carefully-filed collection of newspaper clippings used to drive me to despair. I had neither the patience nor the aptitude to do the same – but I knew I should have. It is important to realize how small are the circulation of academic journals, and the small number of readers are almost always other academics. In taking critical stances one is simply not addressing the world with a loud-hailer from a rooftop. Even in Robert Mugabe's Zimbabwe of the 2000s, it is possible to dissent extensively in academic publications. His regime will take notice if, as a foreign scholar living in Zimbabwe, you graduate to international journalism and broadcasting. It is not that dissent is impossible. Size of audience is the determinant.

So it is surprising that Botswana, a country with high marks for electoral democracy, should quite suddenly lose toleration for the 72 year-old Ken Good. His style has changed not at all in the last 20 years – except that his shock of white hair is even whiter and more unkempt. As professor of political studies at the University of Botswana Ken Good delivered, in February 2005, a seminar paper entitled, 'Presidential Succession in Botswana: No Model for Africa'. This paper had not yet even been published in an academic journal, and the audience for a university seminar is tiny. The paper argued that Botswanan

President Mogae ignores the electorate and has already chosen his own successor. The electorate in any case gives Mogae's party sufficient ethnically-based support for it to remain in power for many years to come.

Good made four key points: that the Botswanan presidency is in fact a sovereign presidency, and that it is answerable neither to parliament nor the cabinet; that minority ethnic groups such as the *San*, the so-called Kalahari Bushmen, are being displaced with impunity; that high *per capita* income figures disguise a significant gap between rich and poor and that much social injustice occurs; and that the style of Mogae's presidency is one of fiat without even superficial note of checks and balances.

In choosing his own successor and ignoring a (largely compliant) electorate, Mogae has been indulging in a form of 'insider trading' without any need to worry about the 'retail politics' of genuine electioneering.

On 18 February, Good was served with a deportation order as being a threat to national security, in his words 'all by myself' (*Times Higher Educational Supplement*, 27 May 2005). I imagine he would have been simultaneously flattered and shocked. He immediately appealed to the courts. This was where the tragi-comedy began – in a way Alexander McCall Smith might never capture – for the attorney-general remarked in court that Botswana was a respected, conservative and small democracy – that did not embrace *avant-garde* rights to freedom of expression recognized by larger countries. The attorney-general then progressed from inconsistency to hysteria. In supporting the deportation of Good he said that the government 'did not want Baader-Meinhof or al-Qaeda in Botswana'.

Despite the outrage of Botswanan newspapers and much of civil society, Good lost his appeal and was deported. The legal grounds for deportation were dubious. The right to freedom of expression is enshrined in the constitution; moreover, various provisions in the Immigration Act violate the constitution and should have no effect; and the entire affair had been procedurally ungrounded. It was pretty much exactly a presidential fiat. Mogae, by his over-reaction, simply provided the evidence for Good's claim. For once, Ken Good did not need to collect newspaper clippings. He was the clipping – but the nature of Botswanan democracy had been called into question, and that question was now, by the president's action, broadcast internationally – somewhat far beyond a seminar room or even the readership of an academic journal. The Good case makes an interesting comparison with one surrounding Roy Clarke in Zambia a year earlier.

The elephant vs Roy Clarke

Roy Clarke had also been a colleague at the University of Zambia. An engineer, he improbably wound up in the department of education. But Roy was always improbable – wacky and irrepressible. He was repressible enough to marry locally and became the husband of Zambia's leading feminist, Sara Longwe. Sara's father could not pronounce 'Clarke', so Roy became 'Kalaki', a name he adopted for his satirical columns in *The Post* newspaper. These columns were indeed irrepressible in their scathing humour. But even the former President Frederick Chiluba took them in good heart – despite being represented as a vain, cross-dressing, high-heel wearing, adulterous dwarf thief called 'Kafupi'. Quite frankly, Clarke's depiction of Chiluba was sometimes defamatory but, for all his other faults, Chiluba at least recognized the flattery of being satirized. Not so his successor, Levy Mwanawasa – whom Clarke never managed to defame, and Clarke's satirical renditions of Mwanawasa never reached the heights of his Kafupi period.

Mwanawasa is a very large man. He is not photogenic and his physical habits were, long before Clarke, the subject of Zambian mirth-making. His earlier infirmities left many wondering aloud whether he had the capacity to be president. But president he became, and his record has been mixed. He has certainly impressed himself on the Zambian consciousness and his visual bulk has helped in this. It was this bulk that Clarke seized upon.

Ironically, the offending column about Mwanawasa was not very funny. It was published in *The Post* on New Year's day 2004 – when most people would be recovering from hangovers rather than trooping downtown to buy a newspaper. The Great Elephant Muwelewele, with his dishevelled safari suit and huge belly hanging over his trousers, is very recognizably Mwanawasa. The gist of the column was a comment on venality, self-interest and constant air-travel instead of the hard work of government. None of this was unusual among the complaints of Zambia's citizenry. What clearly rankled was the elephantine metaphor and Clarke was served with a deportation order.

What followed was a soap opera as Clarke appealed to the courts; the police held his daughter and, when Clarke went to secure her release, he was arrested for assaulting the officer commanding the police station. The government now had him on a 'back-up' charge, and he could be deported as an antisocial person even if he won his original appeal. The credibility of the assault charge was slight, however, slighter when one took the exceptionally weedy frame of Clarke into account. Roy's capacity to swing a punch without falling over is negligible. The courts dismissed the assault charge and upheld Clarke's appeal against the deportation order. What is of interest, however, is the clear legal reasoning of the court's decision against deportation. In a lengthy judgment, which *The Post* printed in full over several pages, it reiterated Clarke's right to free expression, and the need for proper procedure and grounds for deportation. It was, in short, a judicial statement to do with rights, including the right against arbitrariness on the part of the state and its government.

The Clarke case differed from the Kenneth Good case that followed a year later in Botswana. Unlike Good, Clarke had published his satire in Zambia's largest newspaper, with electronic access available around the world. It was similar to Good's in that British newspapers took an interest but, whereas Good was given two pages in the academic newspaper, the *Times Higher Educational Supplement*, Clarke became the cover-boy of the mass-circulation *Guardian* newspaper's G2 magazine supplement. The persecution of both simply broadcast the situation more widely. The resolution of the two cases differed markedly, however. The judicial process in Zambia was manifestly sounder than that in Botswana, emphasizing a clear independence from the president and his executive powers and affirming a check and balance to them. In Botswana, the presidential fiat was felt to have reached into the courts. Clarke, cheekily but well within his rights, continued to write about Muwelewele and, when last sighted, the blundering elephant had not yet begun his diet. *The Post* increased the space given to the Kalaki column, and it must be said that, in order to fill it, some of Roy's latest pieces are silly rather than satirical. His audience had been falling before the deportation order and, if anything, the government effort against him elevated him from side-show gadfly to the resident national critic – in not-unrelated West African terminology, the 'trickster' of Zambia, the uncensorable jester of the political pack. But there is a real difference to be emphasized between Zambia and Botswana for, in strict electoral terms, Botswana has the better international democratic reputation. Mwanawasa's 2001 electoral victory was mired in controversy and subsequent opposition appeals to the courts did substantiate the murkiness of much electoral practice. The Supreme Court of Zambia delivered its verdict in February 2005 and, over five days, *The Post* printed the entire judgment covering 40 tabloid pages and the cautious nature of the verdict was evident in the 'partially proved' statement, and that describing the elections 'not being totally perfect'. The opposition was also found to have had 'reasonable cause for petitioning the election'. Nevertheless, on overall terms, the courts found for the government and upheld its victory. Again, the court's judgment was probably sound, but enough had been put forward as evidence to suggest that not all is well in Zambian electoral democracy. Yet, in the matter of constitutional rights and the protection of the dissident individual – not to mention the capacity of the courts to engage in publicly scrutinized legal contemplation – Zambia is more democratic in its everyday life than Botswana would seem to be. Yet the international community focuses almost entirely on elections.

Here, the report of the Commission for Africa does provide an exception. It calls for a strong constitution in African countries, one that separates the 'powers of the judiciary and

legislature from the executive'. In the same paragraph, however, it immediately sets about at least partially excusing Africa
itself. 'In many cases this balance was lost at independence and
power was consolidated in the executive' (Chapter 4.3.2 para.
51). This appears to say that the constitutional legacy
bequeathed by the departing colonial powers was too weak. If
instead it is saying that, at independence, executives immediately sprang up that were stronger than all other institutions,
then this is untrue. In almost every case, some years passed
before the drift to executive supremacy was truly enshrined –
and this was in the midst of weaknesses in *all* public institutions, and the declared need to address them from the basis of
a strong executive.

Whatever the Commission meant, its report does go on to
say that African presidents should not stay beyond their constitutional terms, and there is a veiled implication that venality
prompts some to seek extensions to their time in office (4.3.2
para. 52). But, almost as if reforming presidentialism was a lost
cause in Africa, the report calls for independent parliaments –
something to hedge the president about. The report is, by now,
rushing and not devoting proper consideration to issues that it
fleetingly raises – sometimes gratuitously. It makes the politically correct and desirable recommendation that there should
be more women MPs; but it does so on the basis that there is
'evidence that corruption falls as the proportion of parliamentary seats held by women rises' (4.3.2 para. 54), but there
is in fact no such evidence applicable to Africa at large; and
one does not have to live long in any African country to hear
vast anecdotes about the failings of female as well as male MPs.

Having said that, the Commission is correct in seeing the
issue of constitutionalism as key, and the related issue of a

judiciary able to enforce the constitution, irrespective of executive wishes, as essential. In this latter yardstick at least, Zambia emerges with higher marks than Botswana.

Is democracy the same as integrity? Some case studies

I visited Ghana in 1981, shortly before the second coup of Flight Lieutenant Jerry Rawlings. He had briefly seized power in 1979 and set about restoring a democracy that, after his departure, was patently not fulfilling the expectations of the voters. Corruption was rising rapidly and nakedly. Rawlings had, I am sure, intended to take a back seat in Ghanaian affairs – being preoccupied with his own youth and dashing image, tooling about the battered streets of Accra in his open-top MG, aviator shades firmly on. In many ways he was an Errol Flynn character. He was even half-Scottish, but his charisma and, above all, sense of integrity made him an idol in the back-streets of the capital. Tooling around those same backstreets in a 4-wheel drive I was less skilful and, of course, trapped myself in a significant pothole. My companion went for help and, the car being immovable by even intrepid thieves, I wandered the streets, becoming the local spectacle. I took shelter in a bar-ber's shop and, with everybody else, waited for my hair to be cut. The barber had never cut straight hair before, and never long straight hair, so he produced a punk look that was both original in Accra and unintended. But I suffered the hedge-pruning of my greatest vanity because the conversation at the barber's was riveting. A small photograph of Rawlings decor-ated the edge of the mirror. If the authorities did not know a second coup was coming, everyone at the barber's shop did. And they wanted it to come. They believed in the young man.

Richard Jeffries, writing very shortly after the second coup, attributed his popular support to his perceived care for the welfare of ordinary people, his personal integrity, and his public moral integrity. There was not another democratic government in Ghana for years and, even then, it was Rawlings who stood successfully for president. Moreover, he was no natural-born politician and certainly not an economist. He had much to learn, had to take many unpopular decisions, and made many mistakes. Looking back, it is amazing how strong his support-base remained. That he was trying very sincerely, though sometimes ineptly and heavy-handedly, and that he was not enriching himself, meant much to the citizens – even as he gradually lost his handsome features and became jowly. By that time, in any case, he had pretty much mastered an economic way forward – or, rather, had come to realize that his country had no choice but to accept the prescriptions of the World Bank and IMF. Those institutions were determined to make Ghana their success story, but it would take the infliction of much pain; Rawlings, with the advice of his minister of finance, steered a delicate path forward. He simply could not have done what he did without popular belief in his own integrity.

When, in 1992, elections were once again held in Ghana – with Rawlings standing for the presidency – they were hailed by international observers as a great success. They were, however, marred by a range of irregularities such as bribery and restricted coverage of the opposition by an extremely pro-government media. Nevertheless, there is no doubt Rawlings was a genuinely popular victor. Other transitions back to democratic rule have been far more fractious and imperfect.

Rawlings was elected in 1992, continuing a presidency that

would ultimately last until the turn of the millennium. His political party continued to hold the presidency until the elections of 2004. Rawlings governed Ghana for almost two decades, half as idealistic young dictator, and half as elected (still idealistic) strongman. The election that set a landmark, however, in *deposing* a strong long-term president was that in Zambia in 1991. Kenneth Kaunda, the founding prime minister, then president of Zambia was early hailed by sympathizers such as John Hatch as a 'philosopher-king', an epithet he held alongside Tanzania's Julius Nyerere. Both made rather poor philosophers and Kaunda at least made himself a king who overstayed his welcome, ruling from 1964 to 1991. Unlike Nyerere, who wisely retired and pulled strings behind the scene, Kaunda was convinced he should stay on, and on. His problems were to do with economic decline, which he patently could not manage and, as van Donge observed, the withdrawal of church support for his regime – an important withdrawal, as Kaunda's carefully enunciated state-philosophy of 'Humanism' relied upon a religiosity that was mired in a missionary vision of Africa. Lacking complexity in itself, the withdrawal of church support for it, and him, was a key element in the political tide rising against him. I shall return to the 1991 Zambian elections later but, for now, it should be observed that democracy, despite its wave beginning in the 1990s – after 30 years of independence – was still used more as a legitimizing device than one capable of causing governmental change. Part of this was certainly due to divided oppositions, but it was not until the 2000s that presidents and governments actually began to fall and be replaced on a frequent basis – and problems have accompanied many such transitions. They have also meant, as in the case of Zimbabwe, presidents and governments determined to stay in power by rigging elections shamelessly.

The end of the 1990s also saw the demise of Africa's most powerful military dictatorships, most notably in Nigeria. There have been eight military governments in Nigeria, and only four civilian. The discrepancy in numbers is because military governments encountered coups of their own, as one faction or generation rallied against another. The current fourth civilian government is headed by Olusegun Obasanjo – a distinguished statesman abroad and a besieged, though active, president at home, mired in struggles against corruption, economic instability, and ethnic and religious tensions. He himself was head of the country's fourth military government, but had the decency and competence to call elections. Successor military governments equivocated over elections, each promising that one was forthcoming, but each delaying or reneging as the attractions of office proved too great, or remaining only to be overthrown by another military *putsch*.

The Obasanjo military government of 1976–79 was a paradigm of what such a government normally promises to be, seldom is, but was accomplished by Obasanjo probably as well as it ever could be. I shall return to this and to the theme of military governments later. For now, it should be said that he was probably more successful as a military president than as a civilian one. The elections of 1999 and 2003 were imperfect, and anecdotal tales of rigging have become legion. However, the 2003 elections, which Obasanjo won for his second civilian term, was the first in 20 years to be organized and conducted by a civilian administration, and only the third in 43 years of independence. Even then, the presidency was contested by two former military dictators, Obasanjo and Buhari. Many former men in uniforms were elected senators and state governors. In a very real way, every aspiration, venality, policy and planning procedure, triumph and failure of politics was enacted in the microcosm of military life and rule in Nigeria. The military provided a kind of laboratory for the nation. It is perhaps no wonder that the nation chooses to elect people with such experience – notwithstanding the brutalities that military rule also brought. But it can hardly be said that democracy has returned to Nigeria in any pristine form. It may be hailed as such, but it is a hybrid of past practices (and personnel) legitimized by democracy, but also with the capacity to look towards the future. Democracy as a political pluralism, unhedged by ethnicities, corruptions, bullying and local fixing, is still very much a future condition. Past imperfect, perhaps future perfect – Africa has invented a new tense, the present imperfect.

Perhaps the real exemplar of such a present imperfect is Kenya, where civilian government has always succeeded civilian government, but where there have been elections since independence without any possibility of an opposition breakthrough – if indeed, in the early days, there was an organized political opposition at all. It is a different case to that of Zambia, where Kaunda ruled continuously until his overthrow in the first multi-party elections for decades. In Kenya, Moi had succeeded Kenyatta, and had held multi-party elections before the one that led, not to his overthrow (he was retiring anyway), but to the overthrow of the hegemony of his party. Effectively, unlike the direct one-party rule of Kaunda, Moi extended the one-party state by other means. In 1991 the constitutional provision that there should be only one party in Kenya was repealed. However, only four months before the

1992 elections, Moi pushed through legislation that effectively prevented any of the new opposition parties and groupings being able to defeat him. Ostensibly designed to prevent ethnic power bases, the stipulations required a 25 per cent vote in at least five of Kenya's eight provinces. However, it allowed Moi to manipulate ethnic coalitions to his own advantage; the opposition had insufficient time to organize in all the provinces; and, in any case, the opposition was fractious, divided and consumed by egotistical leaders. All these factors allowed Moi to win in 1992 – although the combined opposition took 64 per cent of the popular vote. The picture was repeated in 1997, when the opposition won 60 per cent of the popular vote; yet Moi and his party retained office. To his credit, Moi at least was not seeking to rig the polls to demonstrate that a huge percentage of his people loved him. He was wily enough to win rather than win *and* flatter his vanity.

The 2002 elections were won by an opposition that was, frankly, dominated by many deserters from Moi's party. They established a coalition and it was this coalition that was able to organize in every province. In a tangible if not reliably durable sense, the ethnic factor was transcended in the 2002 polls. However, the new president, Mwai Kibaki, had been a staunch party man under both Kenyatta and Moi. He had been Kenyatta's minister of finance and Moi's own vice-president. As with former military officers in Nigeria, Kibaki represents a recycling of the old – albeit with far greater prospects for future change than earlier regimes would allow. Insofar as the 2000s represent an epochal change in the possibility of a politically plural Africa, it is a real but imperfect possibility. It tends to be hailed on the basis that 'something is better than nothing', and it probably is. However, the scale and extent of corruption and poverty in Kenya remain immense, as does the gap between rich and poor. In that sense, Kenya emulates Nigeria, as does the increasing violence and crime that mediates between rich and poor. A quick inspection of the walled streets of Nairobi's elite suburbs, mansions locked behind gates, is always chillingly amusing. The *asgaris*, the unarmed security personnel who guard the fortresses housing plasma screen televisions and designer wardrobes, the possessions of the *wa Benzi* – the ethnically transcendent tribe of the Benz people – have truncheons and night-sticks, are poorly trained to use them and are simply poorly paid. And when the thieves come with their automatic machine guns, they rightly run away. The rich want security, the poor want economic justice. At least these wants and needs can be transacted in a slightly more open society and, again at least, the open possibility of change does lessen the recourse to military takeovers with their inaugural promises, which only a handful, like Rawlings, can ever be said to have kept in mind; and even he never actually kept them as he had first promised them.

The military condition

In a rough and ready division of the continent, southern Africa has been free of military governments, except insofar as liberation movements became the rulers and, to one extent or another, remained militarized. Certainly, all of Anglophone southern Africa has never known military rule. Uganda is the exception in the Anglophonic east. Otherwise, all the Francophonic states of eastern and central, and much of western Africa have had military governments, Senegal being the significant exception. The two major Anglophonic West African states, Ghana and Nigeria, have both had histories of military coups and governments; and, in Sierra Leone and particularly Liberia, there has been the advent of a form of ritualistically brutal and brutalizing military adventurism that has captured the state – professing a cultural formation (or deformation) and mobilizing young shock troops around compressed traditional rituals. I shall return to the Liberian case later, but should observe for now that it is not internationally new in its outline. The Chinese 'boxer uprising' at the beginning of the 1900s deployed tens of thousands of young fighters who, after very abbreviated and somewhat imaginative 'magic' training, graduated as kung fu experts or 'boxers' and sought to storm the foreign strongholds of Peking. They too, like their Liberian successors, adopted magic to make themselves invulnerable, and were given to indiscriminate and gratuitous slaughter of their enemies. Almost every so-called traditional kung fu style of today in fact emanates from the bastardized training of that period. I have overdrawn the analogy, but it introduces a basic point – that, in China, other parts of east Asia, Latin America, and Europe, the twentieth century was one of military rule jostling with civilian rule. Africa may have reached its military moment at the wrong end of the century (as did Greece, Portugal and Turkey) but, in many ways, was unexceptional.

Even so, military rule is by definition hierarchical and autocratic. It is accompanied by military discipline and disciplining, and this can rapidly become abusive and nationally oppressive. Because the military government is armed and effectively monopolizes firepower, dissent is difficult and dangerous. If the military government takes a liking to power and its fruits, it has the instruments to coerce its citizens into subjects and stay in power for very long times. If, in addition, the military president is a buffoon, as were Amin in Uganda,

Bokassa in the Central African Empire, Doe in Liberia, then an unconscionable rapaciousness and arbitrariness can be added to the list of shortcomings. I do not want to dispute any of this. I am very glad that the era of military governments seems to be drawing to a close in Africa. There is something to be said, however, for other dimensions in such rule.

Although a fierce critic of military rule, the distinguished Nigerian novelist, Chinua Achebe, could draw a sympathetic portrait of such a ruler. In his *Anthills of the Savannah*, the young officer/politician, probably modelled after General Yakubu Gowon (the second military president of Nigeria, 1966–75, who waged the civil war to its completion and then made a name for himself as a leader of national reconciliation, afterwards taking a Ph.D. as a normal student at Warwick University), is fellated for the first time. His girlfriend is white and he is both shocked and delighted, not even knowing that such a practice existed. It is a moment of boyish innocence more usual among 17 year-olds – but he is a power in the land. The innocence, naivety and idealism might just as well have applied to Ghana's Jerry Rawlings or Burkina Faso's Thomas Sankara. Insofar as Achebe's character was probably drawn after Gowon, it is amazing that such a relatively sympathetic figure as Gowon did not become the stereotype of African military presidency. Handsome, dashing, and certainly at first a good president, Nigeria's reconciliation after its civil war owes much to his wisdom. Idealism and wisdom could probably also be attributed to his military successor, Murtala Muhammed (1975–76), who was assassinated, and Olusegun Obasanjo (1976–79), who completed the transition to democratic civilian rule first mooted by his predecessors. Obasanjo was the least physically attractive of this line of three, and the 'star quality' of his government owed much to his dashing lieu-tenants, Brigadiers Yar'Ardua and Garba. Even now, in his second incarnation as a civilian president, Obasanjo comes across as burly, laboured and inarticulate. What the apartheid president, P. W. Botha, thought of him when Obasanjo co-led the Commonwealth Eminent Persons Group to South Africa in 1986, in an unsuccessful bid to negotiate an end to minority rule, is anybody's guess. But those who know him well say he is as sharp as a knife. Certainly, the steps he and Murtala took to return Nigeria to democratic civilian rule remain a model today.

1. New states were created in 1976. In the Nigerian situation this was important, as it broke up the concentration of largely ethnic power bases in what had been three large geographical areas. The new number of 19 states was a geo-political attempt at plurality.
2. A new constitution was drafted in 1976 by 50 lawyers, academics and businessmen.
3. Local government was reorganized and local elections, without political parties, took place.
4. Elections for a constituent assembly took place and this assembly debated the draft constitution before dissolving itself in 1978.
5. Political parties were then allowed to be formed, their agendas not having been able to disrupt or influence the constitution.
6. State elections were held.
7. National elections were held and civilian rule was reintroduced in 1979.

It was one of those militarily precise timetables, and bespoke a precision that Nigeria has not seen again. Certainly, arriving at Lagos International and lining up at passport control in that era was an exercise in the straightest possible queues, flanked by soldiers on either side. That precision never addressed the poverty and crime that beset the country, nor checked the rising corruption, but it was a rare moment of order in the public institutions of the country. In part it explains Obasanjo's acceptability to the electorate as a civilian candidate years later. This is of course to tell only part of the story. He was also acceptable to the military establishment – who had by then learnt ways of protecting its self-interest behind the scenes. But behind the scenes is where it was, and the foreground election made much of Obasanjo's technical capacity as a president.

There has been a large body of scholarship that has set about attempting to decipher why military governments appear and how they work, whether they are successful, and why they are often not. The attempt to theorize an entire continent's experience, where there are so many levels of state and national development, and so many types of army, has not really been successful. Pioneering works by Ruth First and Sam Decalo were ambitious efforts to present an overall picture of the military phenomenom. Robin Luckham worked by contrast on an in-depth sociology of the Nigerian armed forces, although he too later published a (brief) overview of the issue. However, the 'classic' writers on military coups in Africa were people like William Gutteridge and Samuel Finer (although Finer wrote about coups internationally). Central to their approach was the assumption of a strong military in a weak society, with weakness behaving like a vacuum, sucking in the strong. Here, the problem is one of low-level development, and not just military agency. The problem is that, very often, there existed both a weak society and a weak military – one mirroring the other. Samuel Huntington, 40 years before his *Clash of Civilizations*, wrote of the military abhorrence of disorder. Certainly the fetish of order was apparent in Obasanjo's countdown to democratization (not to mention the airport queues) but, if that were all a military government could bring, its attraction would have been limited. It had to justify itself by bringing benefits, much as any other government would. Rawlings did that and Obasanjo did that. But it would be best to say that no single body of attributes and reasons fully explains why Africa saw so many coups. What I have been trying to say here is that not all of them have been led by figures like (the British-sponsored) Idi Amin. Some arose as an original phenomenom and provided original service.

Bases for democracy

It was in the wake of Amin that I entered Uganda in the early 1980s, both to help reconstruct a derelict government ministry and to witness the formal end to an insurrection in the Ruwenzori Mountains – what the explorer Speke called 'The Mountains of the Moon' – site of a derelict ski lift on the African equator. We carried several briefcases of banknotes, the currency being almost but not quite value-free, huge drums of our own petrol, and I think I carried with me that peculiar naivety, that confidence that the youthful fiction of invulnerability brings. After all, bullets never hit the centre of the universe. I had permed my long hair, had cultivated a long moustache; I looked, I thought, like Carlos Santana but I must have looked astounding at military roadblock after roadblock, manned by God knows which terribly adolescent soldiers from which army faction or subfaction. We were tracked all through the mountains by armed men in the shadows of every turn in the road. They were carrying an awful lot of hardware not being surrendered at the ceremony to mark the end of that little local conflict. But all through that long trek in Uganda I encountered the ruins of buildings where battles had been fought with the liberating Tanzanian army – or rather where the Tanzanian army had blasted Amin's resistance to smithereens. Marabou storks – they look like vultures on stilts – pecked in every ruin. They even sat on the roof of the parliament building in Kampala, looking ominously down, examining us as morsels.

It was the human accounts that made this journey the defining one of my African life. Uganda was a terribly Anglophone country. School education faithfully replicated the metropolitan curriculum. But some learning is universal. At shattered walls I would come across graffiti, lines from Yeats: 'Things fall apart, the centre cannot hold.' That line became the centre of recitation competitions among my ministry colleagues. All could recite the entire poem. I thought of the marabou storks turning and turning 'in the gyre' (none of us knew what that word meant). People knew about the beast slouching towards Bethlehem. They basically knew Yeats back to front. Something in his writing had touched them, and they turned his most famous lines into scatological humour. At one site we had one toilet, for which I held the one key. I have never had such power again. 'Stephen, *please* let me use the toilet. My centre cannot hold! And things will fall apart!' This would always elicit huge laughter from everyone, and the subsequent sounds of boulders crashing into water would have the line reiterated. 'You see, that is his centre falling apart.' 'It will be the plumbing that cannot hold!' More laughter. It was rather grim laughter. Many were lucky to be alive. The word was 'picked'. If Amin's people came and 'picked' you, you were being led away to death. I visited the execution sites, imagined the barbarities. But these people who had been so close to it all, who considered themselves blessed to be alive – though surly to be alive under such poor conditions – had this constant borrowed refrain of 'the centre cannot hold'. What is this centre?

There is another story of an English poem, an interminably long one – but, like all colonial schoolboys in the 1950s I had learnt all 70 stanzas of Macaulay's Victorian epic, *Horatius*, by heart. The same had happened in South Africa. On Robben Island, the prisoners of apartheid were often subjected to regimes of silence. The only time they could speak was when one of their comrade inmates had died, and they would be gathered at the burial. Then they jointly recited *Horatius*. Of course, the mythology is now that they recited perfectly all 70 stanzas. Maybe they did. We all could in a former generation. But they recited two stanzas in particular. Horatius volunteers to defend Rome with two comrades. The three will fight at the neck of a narrow bridge across the Tiber. While they hold the bridge, the townsfolk will destroy it so that the invading Etruscan army cannot cross into Rome. The three men were about to face 90,000.

And straight against that great array
Forth went the dauntless Three.
For Romans in Rome's quarrel
Spared neither land nor gold,
Nor son nor wife, nor limb nor life,
In the brave days of old.

Then none were for a party;
Then all were for the state;
Then the great man helped the poor;
And the poor man loved the great:
Then lands were fairly portioned;
Then spoils were fairly sold:
The Romans were like brothers
In the brave days of old.

There is some sexism of course in such stories – but all the inmates on Robben Island were men, and they thought they were facing insuperable odds. So was Horatius – but he pulled through, and won the respect of the invading General. The thing is that the democratic aspirations of even pompous reformers such as Macaulay, slightly more than 100 years earlier, were very similar to the democratic aspirations of Africa. Macaulay also called for a strong state, above party and sectarian conflict; he called for solidarity; and, what is often missed, he called for an equity in the distribution of land. And he said these things should be fought for against all odds. It is perhaps not such an old-fashioned poem.

But there is a big difference between this borrowing from Western literature and a determined Western berating of Africa. The new millennium has brought with it an ill sounding acronym, NEPAD. It sounds like a skater's knee pad, it actually means New Economic Partnership for Africa's Development. It is a Tony Blair favourite and it is crudely a money for votes scheme. Become democratic and we will send you more aid. It is addressed to governments and is a call to reform themselves. Thabo Mbeki of South Africa has fought, somewhat desperately, to claim some African ownership of

what would otherwise be an imposition. Africans will be res-
ponsible for their own democratic scrutiny, namely states will
watch one another – but Mbeki's constant watching, and
inaction, over Zimbabwe has not helped lend credibility to the
African component of NEPAD. The whole 'partnership' is West
to Africa, top down, election centred, and prioritizes not at all
the popular African longing for a secure and equitable centre,
one that will not 'pick' its citizens, one where the citizens will
indeed pick the government, but not under the direction and
bribery of another camped at its gates and bridgeheads. I shall
return to the popular foundations for an African future in my
final chapter.

Ngugi used Yeats in his great novel, *Petals of Blood*. The
theme of slouching towards Bethlehem runs through the entire
work and, indeed, is the title of Part Two. After his English
novels, Ngugi began writing only in Kikuyu. Perhaps his
search for authentic expression mirrored a verse from Yeats.

All day I'd looked in the face
What I had hoped t'would be
To write for my own race.

Before that he had used Walt Whitman as an epigram to *Petals
of Blood*.

The people scorn'd the ferocity of kings...
But the sweetness of mercy brew'd destruction,
And the frighten'd monarchs come back;
Each comes in state, with his train – hangman,
Priest, tax-gatherer,
Soldier, lawyer, lord, jailer, and sycophant.

There is an ahistoricism in the foundations of NEPAD. It was Britain that allowed Amin to be visited upon Uganda, France that stood aside in Rwanda, the USA that fostered civil war for decades in Angola, the West in general that ensured the long-evity of apartheid South Africa; that supported long numbers of regimes with their hangmen and jailers and whose banks and coffers have benefited from an African debt that has crushed so many. It may be that it is not in the West where the bases and parameters of democracy should be specified.

Chapter 5
Endless disease

Malaria was the scourge of Africa before HIV. There are some parallels. For years at the university teaching hospital in Lusaka, treating and teaching with or without running water, the overworked doctors would routinely diagnose every otherwise unexplained death as from malaria. These days, without too much testing before death or postmortems after, they are from whatever disease is palatable to the grieving relatives, but the medical assumption is that the symptoms were by-products of HIV. These 'clinical' assumptions, and the seemingly arbitrary assumptions in extrapolating from samples, can throw up bewildering percentages of how many in any given country are HIV-infected. They have come down now from the wild days of up to 80 per cent, but there is no doubt, no matter how unreliable the figure-work, that HIV is the great public health problem of the continent. It is probably a fair UN estimate to suggest that almost 40 million people in Africa are HIV-infected.

But it is not the only disease that ravages Africa. Malaria has not gone away, and drug-resistant varieties are apparent. Tuberculosis is everywhere. Polio is still active. River blindness and forms of leprosy occur in isolated areas – and highly dangerous, highly contagious outbreaks of ebola continue to surface particularly in Congo.

Disease gains its footholds in conditions of poverty. Not only is there the question of hygiene, for example whether clean water is available, but one of personal capacity to resist disease. The more malnourished a person, the more prone he or she is to infection. De Waal studied the famine of 1984–85 in Darfur, Sudan. It was the same famine that attracted so much attention to Ethiopia. Food was belatedly sent to Darfur, but de Waal reports that what was really needed were medicines to prevent the worsening of disease. In Darfur, disease killed more people than hunger. There may have been some chicken and egg there. The infections had their entry point because of weakness caused by hunger. The trick is to be able to deliver food and medicine simultaneously. Even so, as Amartya Sen wrote 25 years ago, it is not a case of there not being enough food. It is that, in every case he studied, people starved because they were not *entitled* to food, that is could not afford to buy it or were politically disadvantaged from obtaining it. In Robert Mugabe's present-day Zimbabwe, the political distribution of food to party-supporters only makes a case in point. And, looking at Zimbabwe, the actual spread of fatalities from AIDS and AIDS-related diseases, despite a very high rate of HIV infection, only grew to alarming proportions when the economy disintegrated in the 2000s and people could no longer feed themselves.

Here I have been as guilty as any in a fruitless effort to help. I was directing money to pay for a student's enrolment on an antiretrovirals programme. The money was earmarked. I did not want him paying off his debts with it and ignoring his health. But, when he died, it was found there was no food in his house. I should have paid for food as well as medicine. The frontline fight against disease in Africa has to be the fight

80

against poverty, but also the politics that cause poverty. This involves international politics as well, and I shall return to this.

In the meantime, the march of many diseases continues to trample its way across Africa. At one time I counted, but when I got past 20 friends, colleagues and students who had died of AIDS-related illnesses I could not bear to keep records any more. Before that it had been malaria, particularly cerebral malaria, that is malaria of the brain. For years I myself had recurrent malaria; and, in all my travels, I never once bathed in the rivers and lakes of Africa for fear of contracting snail-borne infections that corrode the kidneys and liver. All that natural beauty and all that pure waste of human lives! Some were the most beautiful people I have ever known.

The Commission gets its diagnosis right

The report of the Commission for Africa rightly begins its section on health with a disquisition, not on HIV, but on healthcare systems generally. A system that cannot provide antibiotics for minor infections cannot provide antiretrovirals for HIV. What the report does not enter is the debate on entitlement. If health systems do improve, but slowly, how are the small improvements to be distributed? In Zambia I watched the spectacle of two friends, both with mothers suffering from cancer. Both trooped daily across town, paying over the odds at both official outlets and blackmarket suppliers, seeking things as simple as dressings and as unsimple as drugs – not even drugs to treat the disease, but drugs to dull the pain. The central hospital could not supply anything. Quite simply, the mother of the richer friend survived and entered remission. I do not think my other friend ever quite recovered from watching his mother die in awful pain and the helpless surroundings of a dirty central hospital – and has been a driven man for almost 20 years. These days in Zambia you can get whatever you like at the private clinics. You do not have to put it together yourself from the blackmarket. You still have to have money though. And the central university teaching hospital has not improved very much.

Manifestly, the public health system cannot do everything by itself. Health programmes by NGOs are invaluable. The gentle cautioning of the Commission's report is apt. 'However, impact has been greatest where (the NGO programmes) integrate with public health systems' (Chapter 6.2.1 para. 37) because often NGOs seek to go it alone, not only because the public health provision is derelict in the location of the NGO's project, but because auditors back home will want to see a self-contained project. If it is self-contained, it is measurable, it represents money able to be accounted for. Restoring even part of a public health system takes time and money with little immediately to show for it.

The NGOs have got better. When the AIDS pandemic was first becoming impossible to ignore in Zambia I came across a visiting US consultant. He was reporting home on where his group could make a contribution. He lamented the 'impossible lack of public education' on the part of the government to do with HIV-awareness. He had seen no posters or newspaper advertisements, heard no programmes being broadcast. I asked if he understood any of the local languages, and he said 'no'. I pointed out very gently that Zambian vernacular radio was plugging the HIV message constantly, and that he had better 'unmetropolitanize' himself. One group that has, and is the shining example of external medical intervention is Médecins Sans Frontières, but this is an emergency-response provision, and getting everyday public health rehabilitated will take a similar but less spectacular and more protracted intervention that marries what it can bring with what is already, imperfectly, on the ground.

When it comes to HIV, the need for integration is massive. 'It is essential that treatment and care for HIV and AIDS is provided through health systems and not yet another parallel approach that will undermine health care in Africa' (6.2.4 para. 59). It is, however, in one of the Commission's most definitive recommendations that the greatest number of problems arise. 'The international community must reach a global agreement in 2005 to harmonize the disparate response to HIV and AIDS. This must be in support of bold and comprehensive strategies by African governments that take account of power relationships between men, women and young people' (6.4.3 para. 88). There are two major problematic aspects to this recommendation. The first is to do with harmonization and the second is to do with power relationships that, in fact, go far beyond men, women and the young. I shall comment on each aspect in turn.

Harmonization

Visiting embassies in the capitals of Africa is always a sobering experience. The mechanics of representation are laborious and resource-consuming. After the bombings in Nairobi and Dar es Salaam, the US embassies are increasingly fortresses. They always had marine guards and their own commissaries – where all the supermarket goodies of Iowa could be purchased cheaply – but now they are citadels. At least their personnel live in houses spread over town. The Chinese, by contrast, house all their people on-site. Their citadels are communities.

One need never see a 'native' unless the creature is invited in. The British variety is punctuated by lockable, padded doors in the corridors. Unlike the US citadels, the British ones can be stormed; you just cannot get very far once inside. Even the smallest embassy follows a pattern. You get into the vestibule if you get past security at the gates. Depending on the importance of your visit, or the recognized importance of your person, you will be seen in the vestibule, in an ante-chamber to the vestibule, in a minor office, in a conference room, finally in the ambassador's chambers. There you will make teeth-grindingly small talk, usually with a political appointee who has no interest in Africa. At least even the most moronic French ambassador will whip out some decent wine if you charm him by your wit (and irony).

They follow a pattern too in resource distribution. Aid monies have to be channelled into programmes and projects that bear the donor's national stamp and that will satisfy the donor's accountants. The monies will go to the latest politically fashionable causes. Right now, that includes HIV. The problem is that NGOs will follow exactly the same pattern of aid disbursal. There must be a self-contained stamp on it. Not only that, it will follow metropolitan protocols. So take HIV/AIDS: the first step is to consult interested groups, those that can help deliver the programme – seldom the patients – and the consultation is about how the delivery agents will fit into the protocols declared as necessary back home; the second step is to provide logistical support, usually vehicles so that the programme can have outreach; the third step is to hold a training workshop, so that all the delivery agents will know what to do, and what they must do is administer their programmes on a regulated basis, namely the patient receives care on condition

84

he or she undertakes to be regulated as well as treated by the programme; each of these steps is accompanied by as much publicity as can be generated in the local media; finally, the programme is meant to be implemented. At which stage it encounters a variety of problems, to which I shall return.

In the meantime, because there are only so many people suitable to act as delivery agents in any one developing nation, this small group comes to lead a magnificent existence. They drive in their embassy, UN or NGO-provided transport, usually a four-wheel-drive Toyota Land Cruiser or its SUV clone, to a succession of training workshops, where they will be trained in exactly the same way by trainers flown out from whichever country is acting as donor, and they will be accommodated and fed at the usually upmarket hotels that also provide the conference facilities in which the training takes place. Weeks can pass in a round of training workshops and comfortable hotels, driving in comfortable vehicles, without a single patient having received any treatment. And, indeed, the spectacle is scarcely edifying of these same habitual trainees soliciting the 'girls of the night' who linger outside their hotels and, from their own breakfast boasting, *not* diluting their pleasure with condoms. If indeed there were harmonization of the myriad programmes, governmental and non-governmental, this routine would be curtailed and, theoretically, some real work would begin. In what, however, does this real work consist?

There is certainly a community education task, but this must overcome prejudices of a complex nature, and it must deliver follow-up. If the four-wheel-drive SUVs actually penetrate the rural areas, as opposed to cities and towns, there is something as simple but as difficult to overcome as an unavailability of condoms. If the nearest, already under-equipped clinic is an

11-kilometre trek away, and it does not have aspirin let alone condoms, why bother? This is not to castigate the dedication and ingenuity of the clinic workers. I heard of one case where a child with first and second-degree burns all over her body was carried into a clinic that had no antiseptic creams or lotions at all. An ambulance was radioed-for, but it had to come some miles on bad roads from the nearest town. In the meantime, the clinic staff coated the child in toothpaste. And this was just enough to keep her alive until better help arrived. But you cannot improvise a condom. In the rural areas where life can be very harsh, home-brewed alcohol and sex may provide the sole pleasures. The combination is not conducive to precautions. And, if joy now is so sparse and fleeting, why abstain in the hope of a longer dreary future?

As for abstention, there is a worldwide church drive to confront the spread of HIV with chastity or fidelity. This is fine as far as it goes, but many church groups advocate abstinence as a sole strategy. Catholics with an abhorrence of contraception will not view condoms, even if available, as sanctioned protectors against disease. There is, moreover, as part of the churches' own Victorian colonial legacy, a public prudishness about sex that contrasts with the private promiscuity even of many priests, and certainly of politicians and businessmen. The combination of sinfulness and concealment, of taking often constant if furtive pleasure while avoiding detection, of genuine remorse for sinfulness and addiction to a primal pleasure, has led to an impossibility of open debate beyond impersonal terms.

It has also led to the impossibility of Western protocols for the dispensation of ARVs. This is the next stumbling block for anti-HIV programmes, after all the training courses and hotel meals have finally been finished. Someone wishing to enrol in an ARV treatment programme must submit to counselling. Part of this counselling demands that the patient reveal his or her sexual partners, with a view to bringing them in for treatment. But this means exposure of infidelity, and the infidelities of partners; it means the end of marriages and it means that the search for confidential treatment ends, on the grapevine, in great public shame. Added to this may be, in many traditions, a marked reluctance and incapacity to talk about intimacy to strangers – to counsellors – and there is no end of people who have approached programmes for help and then, learning what self-exposure is required, never return. Even if the final step is taken, and a patient is enrolled on an ARV programme of treatment, there is no guarantee that the national supply of ARVs will be regular, or that the generics used will not be ineffectual or, as in at least one ministerial scam, have been purchased cheaply (the difference between price and budgetary allocation having been pocketed by the minister) only to be discovered as past their use-by date. Part of harmonization has to be an across-board guarantee of reliability in both availability and efficacy.

Meanwhile, the public education programmes can be overtaken by political point-scoring. In multiparty democracies, where actual party policies differ very little (the policy options available are very limited), vitriol passes for debate. Politicians will challenge opponents to take public HIV tests. Those issuing the challenges are those who have been earlier tested negative, and they take to task those they know to be at risk of infection. If, under politician A's challenge, politician B proves positive, then all manner of shame may be heaped on his or her head; if politician B refuses to take the public test, all manner of suspicions are heaped in his or her direction, with the bonus of being able to say that he or she is not helping the HIV-awareness campaign. Behind the scenes, those who know they are positive are attending private clinics, using public funds to ensure their longevity at a price their constituents cannot afford. In a way, this is the real nature of power relationships in what is not only an HIV pandemic but an HIV scandal. In this environment, the reluctance of people to come forward for testing may not be only denial – it may be avoidance of public shame. The West acknowledges the meaning of public shame in the Orient, its classical philosophers know how devastating public shame was in ancient Greece; no one seems to acknowledge the need for treatment protocols that grapple with African shame – and the vitriolic uses of shame.

Power and politics

There is certainly a power imbalance between men and women when it comes to, for example, the use of condoms. Preeti Patel has written of the Kenyan situation: 'The male condom is entirely dependent upon men's consent. Many men argue that women who carry condoms with them (or even at times insist upon their use) must be promiscuous or unfaithful since they are so well prepared for sex.' Again, this is the use of stigma, and it is a gendered stigma. Even so, there have been conspicuous rises in condom acceptability. In Senegal the use of condoms rose from 800,000 in 1988 to 9 million in 1997. Having said that, it is estimated that the population of Senegal is just under 9 million, which means that one condom is used per person per year. The two shining examples of government activism in Africa are Uganda, where NGOs have a free hand to launch their programmes (albeit with the drawbacks and duplications noted above) and public education does seem to have had an effect; and Botswana, which has had a national policy on HIV/AIDS since 1993 and has benefited from the huge donation made by Bill and Melinda Gates to fight HIV around the world.

Against that is the marked reluctance of South Africa's Thabo Mbeki to recognize the link between HIV and AIDS, and to devote the resources of a rich nation to the wide availability of ARVs. No one has worked out why Mbeki and his senior officials have refused to acknowledge the situation and act. It is true that the South African economy is a tenuous balancing act, with many calls upon it both nationally and regionally, but the refusal to act on this issue can only compromise the longer-term prosperity of South Africa when large numbers of the work force start to die. The political refusal to act may lead to greater detriment than the political embrace of the HIV cause in order to discredit opponents.

If privately the rich obtain care that is beyond the poor, if priests publicly sermonize about abstinence while furtively keeping mistresses, if men denigrate women as a means of avoiding the use of condoms, if care is available in the cities but not in the countryside, if treatment and counselling protocols are Western-centric and discourage African participation, if young people are the generation left to carry the can as parents die and young girls are subject to predatory advances by older, richer, more powerful men, if politicians talk garrulously about HIV-awareness only to impute shame to their opponents, and if rich governments outright practise denial, then all of these are power relationships that include but go beyond those listed by the Commission for Africa.

There is one further power relationship that does not override, but that should be seen as dominant in the fight against both disease and poverty – and that is in the debt Africa owes to its Western creditors. Poku and Cheru have written scathingly of what massive indebtedness actually means for Africa – in the face of kind words in the West. When Europe spends more annually on ice cream than every penny that Ethiopia can earn – and when structured trade imbalances mean that Africa cannot trade its way upwards; and Tony Blair's much touted 2005 G8 summit did nothing to alter the trading structures of the world – then we see a determination that Africa will remain poor and, even if not quite as poor as before because of such debt cancellations and aid increases that the G8 could muster, then poorer than any other continent on earth. I reiterate my earlier linkage between poverty and disease. So in the next chapter I turn to the question of debt and economics.

Chapter 6
The inhibition of an economic Africa

For the most part Europe did not loot Africa. Loose readings of the Guyanese writer Walter Rodney's famous book, *How Europe Underdeveloped Africa*, have provided a crude picture of a complex process. It was complex enough so that on a strict cash-flow basis Africa often did not 'break even' in terms of the costs of colonialism. Anthony Kirk-Greene's phrase, 'the thin white line', describes a British system of district administrators who were tightly stretched with few resources in reserve. Even the iconographic writer of African despair and uprising, Frantz Fanon, was writing from the perspective of alienation as a psychological attribute of maltreatment. A native of Martinique, like Walter Rodney of Caribbean birth, he 'adopted' Africa by becoming a protagonist of the Algerian revolution. David Macey has given Fanon a context by pointing out that, in both Martinique and Algeria, he was appalled by the immense and brutal condescension of white settlers. But only a minority of African territories became settler states, with umbilical trading links to their homelands. Fanon might well be profitably used today to scrutinize the psychological impulses of Robert Mugabe's war against white farmers but, as with his Zimbabwe so also with Africa's colonial history, direct economic profitability was not the primary aim.

It is possible to enter the other extreme and say that, at the 1884–85 Berlin Conference, Africa was of such little importance that the European powers were able – over Christmas pudding – to carve up Africa among themselves with not a shot being fired and many toasts being drunk. It was a case of accommodating a number of competing imperial dispositions. Harder, more competitive and violent in other cases, Africa at least could be successfully negotiated.

It was all more complex than either scenario of direct plunder or casual drawing of lines on a map. Those lines, even if arbitrary in places, were arbitrary in unimportant places – insofar as all then-current European interests were preserved and formalized. Moreover, although it is simple to dismiss Rodney and Fanon as African *manqués*, Caribs coming 'home', there was an intimate link between Africa and the Caribbean, and not only from the slave trade, which so visibly provided the racial background of all the Caribbean today. Richard Drayton considers the Caribbean plantations to have been extensions of Africa. There was an international economic push and pull involving African slave trading as the foundations of plantation labour, the harvests of Caribbean sugar, coffee, cotton and tobacco (later replicated by white settlers in parts of Africa), and how these commodities transformed the domestic habits and industrial landscape of Europe. The textile industries of Manchester and Liverpool, the lace industry of Nottingham, are all cases in point involving cotton alone. Raymond Williams and Edward Said were perfectly correct to point out that the genteel country life-styles of Jane Austen's heroines could only be set against an industrial and exploitative background. This sort of industrial development spurred on the growth of European banking, insurance, the first commodity speculations – in short, the 'invisible' industries of economic modernity, as well as the heavy industries of factories, which in turn slowly provided the Western world with a social conscience towards its own workers. It has to be said that, isolated examples apart, it took the trade union movement in Britain some time to recognize the labour of Africa and Africans, while defending the labour rights of their own. When, at a later stage, African minerals, especially gold, were discovered, Europe's place in international trade was cemented. Drayton writes that the buying power of the West, invested in Indian projects, allowed Europe to eclipse China at the close of the nineteenth century. I daresay Drayton has underestimated the internal engines of China's decline, but his overall thesis is clear. It was not necessarily that Europe directly plundered Africa (although it did do that when minerals were discovered as a second stage of an imperial project already underway), but that Africa became a key element in a world economy in which the benefits flowed to the West, but not to Africa. By the time of Kirk-Greene's colonial administrators, the entire system of international trade had been established, slavery had served its purpose and been abolished, and the world could get on very well without investing in Africa outside its own settler plantations and the South African, Congolese, and to an extent Ghanaian mines.

Having said that, and leaving aside the separate history of South Africa under protracted apartheid, it must also be said that, at the time of African independence, most of the Western world was undergoing economic difficulties. British society had just about recovered from the Second World War, but its strength was tenuous in the face of new economic conditions. The whole energy of the pop revolution came in some measure from 15 years of austerity, from 1945 to 1960, having been endured and giving rise to a postwar generation that wanted very much to break free from austerity's constraints and values. Even so, the youth revolution took place against the background of Harold Wilson's government in the 1960s needing to devalue the currency and beg from the IMF. The war had wiped out Europe's economic musculature and it was the USA that ruled the capitalist world. There was to be, from Britain at least, no economic legacy to give to the new states of Africa. France did slightly better, but by tying in African economies to the French, so that a true independence was never fully given. But, while Wilson fretted about Britain's gold reserves, it is as well to point out that those reserves were to a large extent bullion extracted from earlier days in South Africa. Such bedrock that the British economy could stand upon owed still to Africa.

Africa's current economic plight owes not so much to the lack of legacy on independence. For the most part, independence came without the inheritance of debt as well. The indebtedness of Africa arises from a fifth stage – after the slave trading, formal colonial, war era and independence stages – and derives from Africa's own rush towards development, but amid an unforgiving capitalist world economy. Ironically, it was the political efforts of Arab states, part of the Non-Aligned Movement alongside Africa, to use oil as leverage against the pro-Israeli policies of the West that saw a spiral of increasing development costs. Increased petroleum prices in the mid-1970s hit directly at the new African states. Simultaneously, the Arab oil producers, now flush with huge increases in income, looked for ways to invest their gains. Western banks were delighted to handle the new 'petro dollars' and loaned them on at cheap initial rates to African countries. The assumption was that a state could not go bankrupt and, as a matter of course, had to be a sound borrower. It is fair to say that banks were quite aggressive as well as seductive in soliciting borrowers. The rates being cheap, the cost of oil having risen, the imperative of faster development being an incentive to states now experiencing political unrest and coups, and the realization on the part of many elites that corruption was quite easy, and the bigger the sums the more opportunity there was for corruption, saw a huge uptake of the new loan monies being made available to African states.

It is hardly necessary to say that there was much foolhardiness. Often, no coordinated records were kept of which government agency had borrowed what from whom, and with what fine print – chiefly to do with possible future variation in interest rates. It is also unnecessary to say that many of the borrowed funds were spent in futile projects, or that much 'commission' found its way into private pockets. It was, in short, the time of squander. When, as in Nigeria, oil was discovered, and no longer needed to be imported but could be sold abroad, a bonanza of economic imprudence and self-enrichment took place, and it can hardly be said that Nigeria's oil-income has benefited ordinary citizens, and that the debt undertaken to make up shortfalls in oil revenues has been wise. Even so, it was not Africa's over-borrowing that was its undoing, but that of Latin America. The international banking crisis of 1982 was because key, large Latin American states threatened not to repay their loans. By this time, in their own brand of recklessness, many Western banks had over-loaned.

Their asset bases could not cope with non-repayment. By the time the crisis was settled, commercial banks would no longer lend vast sums to African countries, or third world countries in general; interest rates for existing loans rose; official government-to-government loans increased and, above all, the IMF became the lender of first resort – with all its packages of conditionality. Economic sovereignty was now lost by the recent politically-sovereign states of Africa and, by this stage, there was no turning back in terms of what development entailed. Development, throughout Africa, was locked into a paradigm of service and ameliorative industries that demanded liquidity flows that Africa for the most part could not itself generate.

This is where for the most part the report of the Commission for Africa is correct. Debt needs to be cancelled, especially as interest payments have exceeded the original capital borrowed. The problem comes with the implementation of debt cancellation. A whole new generation of conditionality is being installed and, to qualify for debt relief, the number of imposed hurdles to be jumped, with auditors watching throughout, means that economic sovereignty is not, for a long time, to be returned to Africa. This is, in effect, the new colonialism: an external power governs your fiscal capacity. This is not to mention what might be called the new imperialism: the outreach of intervention, not by states, but by corporations that will promise employment and build the infrastructures made possible by aid, but will also enrich their own Western shareholders significantly more than their new host countries. It has all become more subtle and complex than colonialism and imperialism once were, and these are perhaps not even suitable labels for phenomena that differ so comprehensively in their global mechanics from those of their predecessors, but they are not completely inappropriate as crude descriptors.

If global, particularly Western interests are at work in Africa (but watch the rise of the Chinese in this game), they are not simply the outreach of 'global capital' or some other crudely formulated term. This outreach was made possible in large part because of the weakness and greed of African leaderships. The history of all this, and the impact of HIV/AIDS, mean that Gertrude Stein's barbed comment, never meant to be applied to Africa – 'you are all a lost generation' – rings truest here. The answer lies in Africa developing its own capacity to help itself. To do that it must be able to trade globally. The greatest failing of the Gleneagles G8 summit of 2005 was the unwillingness of the West, particularly the USA, to contemplate in any concrete terms the liberalization of trade that would allow Africa fair entry into competition. All the recommendations of the Commission for Africa's report in this regard, pretty much all of Chapter 8, were ignored. But, even if they had been accepted, with what would Africa trade? Here the report understates the immensity of what needs to be caught up.

In 2002 the South African public scholar, Greg Mills, wrote a book that largely predated the tenor of the Commission for Africa's report. In that sense, it was all 'out there' anyway. But it was published in South Africa, Geldof would not have read it and, in any case – and this is where someone in show business remains someone who does show business – Geldof, rather expertly, used Tony Blair to make what was already 'out there' into an extravaganza of public concern to which the political establishment was, out of vanity or out of recidivism to earlier idealisms and humanity, willing to be tied. Glamour and poverty make good political bedfellows. The politics would not, however, stretch to the question of trade and, even more, skirted the question of industrialization. For, if Africa is indeed to trade, it cannot make its fortune as an exporter of produce and raw commodities. The Chinese have learnt that. The problem is that the Chinese are already bankrupting European garment manufacturers for instance, by the aggressive export of cheap clothing. Another continent emerging into world competition would not be welcomed. All manner of attendant questions arise at this point: sweatshop conditions, child labour, environmental concerns. And Africa has of course that other image about it – the one that goes with what is essentially Geldof's representation of poverty as picturesque (it *has* to be picturesque in the literal sense, otherwise a visual generation will not 'plug into' it), and that is Africa as the picturesque last frontier of humanity at its bucolic simplest, namely purist, amid nature, amid the provision of 'basic needs' that allow the weaving of beautiful 'native' cloths and stringing of necklaces. This really is not what any sophisticated, even if benighted, people wish to be confined to. Mills collected a variety of data from UN sources, and they reveal that, in any case, there will have to be many steps before the picturesque is endangered.

Some 40 of the 48 sub-Saharan countries have gross domestic products that are lower than the turnover of the five-hundredth company ranked in the 2002 Fortune 500 index, that is below the *lowest* such company – Sodexho Alliance (which has captured the catering outsourcing contracts of many UK universities) – and 'light years' away from the number two on the Fortune 500, which is Wal-Mart. Americans will supermarket much more than any African country can perform economically. The richest sub-Saharan countries, South Africa and Nigeria, would be listed only 27th and 51st on the Fortune 500. A European country as small as Belgium would be ranked eighteenth.

Dwelling on Belgium as a comparator, the combined GDPs of *all* 48 sub-Saharan African countries would equal that of Belgium. Since South Africa and Nigeria would contribute 51 per cent of the African total (South Africa 40 per cent and Nigeria 11 per cent), it means that 46 of the 48 have a combined GNP equivalent to less than half of Belgium's. In population terms, that is 450 million people in those 46 countries, against the ten million of Belgium. And the benefits of that GNP would be distributed considerably more thinly (45 times more thinly) and somewhat less equitably than in Belgium.

Even with all 48 in the count, their combined gross domestic product is less than the expenditure on agricultural subsidies in the 18 richest Western nations.

In terms of trade, the African share of total world trade is only 2 per cent, which is down from the 3 per cent of the 1990s. Taking South Africa out of the equation, Africa's share is 1 per cent. Frankly, this is awful. Its trade share is so low already, and the West will not allow Africa fairer conditions to trade more. In those terms, the G8 at Gleneagles was a disaster.

There are six major conditions that Africa must significantly ameliorate in order to compete internationally, if ever it is allowed to.

1. African countries by and large are exporters of a very narrow range of primary products: the diversification is low and their industrialized component is low, namely they are just that, primary as opposed to manufactured products.

Manufacture automatically increases the chances of diversification and reduces the market vulnerability of just one or two products. For example, when world prices for copper crashed, the Zambian economy had no other major export.

2. Africa is a capital exporter, in other words its indebtedness is huge. It exports funds as interest payments. This has already been laboured by the Commission for Africa and almost all writers on Africa. What it means in addition, however, is that the savings rate in Africa is the lowest in the world. The money all goes outwards. There is very little left for potential investment inwards, and this leads to the third condition.

3. Africa is therefore aid-dependent.

4. All this leads to a structural condition in which Africa is mired in poverty with 40 per cent of the population surviving on US$ 1.00 per day. The human capital required for development will not spring out of this condition. All human capital of this 40 per cent is devoted to subsistence, to survival – somehow.

5. The degradation of the human condition is mirrored and accompanied by the degradation of infrastructure. Aid dependency often means the acceptance of aid that accomplishes a new project, auditable from its beginning to end under a self-contained plan, so the dependency is on the creation of the new and not maintenance of the old. Infrastructure crumbles and agriculture, and such industry as exists, is decapitalized. As they in turn crumble, people lose employment; the community loses financial cohesion and then social fabric, and so on and so on.

6. Insofar as social fabric may be sustained by government budgets for example schools and clinics, these have also

been 'decapitalized' as the IMF has demanded a fiscal discipline that discourages any expenditure without a financially measurable return. The rundown or withdrawal of such social amenities leads to lack of confidence in government and, if government is also seen as self-serving and corrupt, leads to lack of confidence in governmental systems, for example to do with a purportedly national project, if some regions benefit more than others; to do with civilian democracy, if there is no benefit from democracy or the quarrels of civilian politicians; to do even with modernity, if what passes as modern is out of reach and, when it is not, is experienced in the form of weapons and technologized brutalities that terrorize the people.

These are overlapping circles. They are not static, but become overlapping spirals out of control. Africa is not 'found' in any single stable condition, but is a series of vortexes. I do not have the answer to any of the questions posed by the vortexes. I do think we have misunderstood, underestimated, disregarded and ridiculed the response of Africans to impossible conditions and impossible questions. This is a book about the ambiguities and complexities amid the impossible, so we come now to perhaps the greatest site of ambiguities and complexities, and that is the 'backwardness' that is African culture. But I do conclude this chapter with a restatement of what Frantz Fanon was meant to stand for. Some 300 years after the advent of the slave trade, 120 years after the colonial partition of Africa, 45 years after the era of 'independence', and more than 20 years after the introduction of IMF economic intervention, the people of Africa are angry – with their own leaders and systems, and with the world.

Chapter 7

Looking backwards or inventing forwards? The vexed condition of culture and tradition in Africa

W hen Kenneth Kaunda called Zambia a Christian nation, declaring Christianity to be its 'tradition', and called *nshima*, the staple maize meal, traditional food, and went on to describe the *chitenge*, the female wrap skirt, as traditional dress, he was completely wrong on all counts. Unless, that is, he acknowledged the creation of tradition since missionary, settler and colonial times. The introduction of Christianity was the advent of something entirely new and foreign; maize meal was an invention, a food to feed workers cheaply and effectively; the wrap skirt was a missionary idea to enforce the notion of modesty. Kaunda was personally at pains to appear 'traditionally' African. He borrowed Ghanaian dress and, for a time, sported the sartorial style of Kwame Nkrumah – even though such dress had never been seen in Zambia. He devised a 'national philosophy' that emphasized an equitable communalism that derived he said from the old African values and methods of cooperation and mutual assistance. The fact that he added elements of twentieth-century social democracy, welfare statism along the lines of Harold Laski's thought, Ghandian pacificism, and Yugoslav international non-alignment was beside the point – not to mention his later introduction, again under his 'national philosophy', of an East European-style one-party state. All this was, he said, essentially 'African'. It was in fact a bold claim, if a ridiculous one. It ignored the stratifications, the slave trading and slave owning of his own Bemba people only a few hundred years earlier, the practice of Bulozi nobles growing long finger-nails to show they did not need to work (women and slaves did that), and the intercommunal violence and warfare that characterized the history of what is now Zambia.

Kaunda had received a missionary education. From this he inherited a missionary view of historical Africa. John Iliffe has written, after researching early missionary correspondence, that the notion of African communalism and social equality derived in fact from the missionary observation that everyone was poor. From this the legend grew that equality was a tradition in times of wealth as well as poverty. It is important to point out how important the missionary accounts, and mis-understandings – perhaps idealism, perhaps desire to think positively of their new flocks – became. This is because their accounts became the first African *written* historical records and thus became points of reference – to use a fashionable contemporary term, became 'discursive' foundations. The whole search for an African authenticity must disentangle what has become highly syncretic and layered. Mixture after mixture has been laid on top of misconception after misunderstanding, and culture and tradition have become tools to be used in the entire 'imagination' of the new nations. There could not be a modern Africa in its multi-state and nationalist form without a mixture of foundations. To this extent, the efforts of Africana or black studies faculties in US universities, to decipher an authenticity, are doomed to failure – particularly if they continue to extrapolate from cultural examples at random, for example a song from Mali is treated as evidence alongside a bronze sculpture from Benin, alongside stone city ruins in Zimbabwe, alongside the currency system in the Gold Coast of what is now Ghana. The African intellectual, Mudimbe, is absolutely right that there is the need to uncover, recover an African *gnosis*, but this *gnosis*, this exemplary, animating, and foundational knowledge of self, material and transcendent, is not yet discovered.

Kaunda, as he progressed his rule, abandoned Ghanaian dress and affected safari suits. They were meant to be emblems of simplicity, as was the cuisine he ate at State House. European visitors would marvel that the powerful president still ate *nshima*, tomatoes, rape, powdered groundnuts and pumpkin leaves – neglecting to realize that all these except the groundnuts were recent additions to the local diet, or to observe that the food was served on expensive china, or to recognize the label-conscious Kaunda's simple dress consisted of a safari suit from Simpson's in Piccadilly, a cravat and handkerchief from Turnbull and Asser's in Jermyn Street, and a Rolex watch. Sincerity, or the affectation of sincerity, covered a multitude of sins – as did perhaps belief. If you believe it to be true, it is. The tradition is 'true' because people think it is. But this means tradition is fluid enough to be bent to many ends.

In neighbouring Zimbabwe, Robert Mugabe's use of the 'tradition' of uprising, of *chimurenga*, has been turned into a tradition of constant revolution. Insofar as it is a tradition at all, it dates back only to the first great insurrection against white settler rule in the nineteenth century. As one of two appendices to this book I attach an essay on 'endless *chimurenga*' in Zimbabwe. I credit this 'tradition' as a political invention – but, like all sweeping and defiant political inventions, a very clever one. Some of the complexities and nuances of invention have been collected into Leroy Vail's still invaluable book, *The Creation of Tribalism in Southern Africa*, and the title summarizes the proposition that not all that appears primordial actually is.

None of this is particularly unusual. The recorded antiquity of the Chinese should not disguise their origin in numerous nations and disparate peoples. The 'United Kingdom' is scarcely united when it has had to devolve powers to regions that are 'national' – Scottish, Welsh and, with varying political affiliations, Irish. The seventeenth-century novelist, Daniel Defoe, rather trenchantly observed what a bastard race even the 'true-born' English were – Anglo-Saxon, Roman, Norse, Norman – to which could be added French Protestant refugees, Jewish migrants and, even in Defoe's time, African and Indian individuals. Some European imaginations of nationalism have been more successful than others. It has cohered in Germany, mostly in Italy, problematically in Spain – despite all three having been many separate kingdoms – and has not cohered in the former Czechoslovakia and Yugoslavia. Some European nationalisms, such as in Finland, are spectacularly recent, and the language differences in Belgium and Switzerland indicate that there is a politesse of toleration that goes into nationalism. For many years the USA was the ultimate polyglot nation, but contemporary cosmopolitanism now means that almost every Western nation has a mixed ethnic population. The point is that, in all these cases, huge efforts are made to reinforce – if not actually *enforce* – the imagination of one nation: compulsory daily pledging of allegiance to the flag in US schools, compulsory national military service in many European states, and a jingoism at sporting events that is almost Roman in its pitting one competitor against another. Imagination must sometimes be extreme, if accepted as amazingly naturalistic, as in the film *The Magnificent Seven*, where the American fighters are cardboard cutout to be different to the dastardly Mexican *bandido*s, despite the leader of the seven being quite clearly Mongolian.

This extended digression is to illustrate with what artifice the new nations of Africa must survive and develop as nations. There is not too much that was originally homogenous, that has not had to be rallied to a new flag and new senses of identity and organization. The rallying has had to deploy cultural and traditional motifs. Men actually never did wear the kilt throughout Scotland, just as women never wore the *chitenge* in pre-missionary Zambia. Insofar as there are familiar techniques and tactics to almost all nationalisms this is well and good. The outside imagination of Africa, however, is of traditional and cultural animations to do great harm, not only to unified nationhood, but to universal concepts of humanity and sanctity. One terribly graphic example is in Liberia where the curious mixture is not only indigenous but has significant American origin. Even so, the recent civil war has been culturally terrifying.

Liberia

As its name suggests, Liberia was meant to be a place of liberty.

It was where many freed American slaves were 'repatriated', starting in 1822; and the same 'return home', involving former British slaves, saw the rise of Freetown in neighbouring Sierra Leone. The problem was that, in both cases, the 'returnees' were some generations into being American or British. In the case of Liberia, all manner of US artefacts were imported to the new 'free state', a lookalike flag, the currency, public institutions, Baptist Christianity – not to mention secretive institutions such as the Masonic Lodge (which had played a major role in the move away from archaic thought in the eighteenth-century Enlightenment), and a name for what became the dominant political party, but borrowed from British liberalism, the True Whigs.

The existing inhabitants, usually living inland from the coast and the new city of Monrovia, were marginalized and regarded as savages. They were all loosely called Krahn, although they spoke a variety of languages and dialects, but they were generally the outsiders and untouchables of their own land. Such tribal identities as they had up till then became sharpened as they sought an organized means either of preserving their own cultures, or not being overwhelmed by the new Americanized culture. Syncretic belief systems soon grew up. These were part of the normal processes of adaptation. However, the new rulers of Liberia also had to adapt. As a species of American-style elections developed, presidents and senior politicians had to appeal for votes in the hinterland by appearing as much one of 'theirs' as a neo-Bostonian Brahmin. For a while it could be said that Liberia was a laboratory of cultural miscegenation, except that the freed slaves and their descendants kept power firmly in their own grip. Their control of the political processes, patronage and all important institutions – public or private – gave them huge leverage in all things requiring 'popular' support.

In a way, Liberia is an example of what can happen when blackness alone is the identifying mark of Africa and African diaspora. There are nevertheless the other markers of political organization, economic power, and a disdain for the techno-logically 'primitive'. A culture of superiority and condescen-sion accompanies political, economic and technological power when these attributes are markers of a minority among 'heathens' and 'savages'. This was rather freely admitted by the first great pan-Africanist and black solidaritist, Edward Blyden. The imposition of new norms was for the protection of the natives – even if only from predatory outsiders who wished to subvert the freed-slave state. Only recently rediscovered by Africana and black studies, Blyden came to Liberia via the USA from the Caribbean. He also founded the university college in Fourah Bay, Sierra Leone, and wrote of a free and intellectually founded blackness. He was, in any sense, an exceptional figure, boundless in his energy and idealism, but he probably gave as much endorsement to the Americanization of Liberia as he brought intellectual freedom to Africa. His Liberian heirs, as late as the 1960s – when independence was being won all around them – wore topcoats at ceremonial functions, three-piece suits to the office (Monrovia is *very* hot), danced to Tamla Motown and despised 'native' music. Meanwhile, Nkrumah was wearing traditional dress in Ghana, Kaunda was imitating him in Zambia, and even the highly Francophile Senegalese president, Senghor, was introducing African speech rhythms into his internationally-acclaimed poetry. More tell-ingly, independence was being won in Kenya with a significant role being played by the Mau Mau insurrection, an animation of indigenous thought turned to rebellion and terror. Those being deprived of all else will reach inside themselves and their cultures and recreate, perhaps create, a foundation for their own rising.

In 1980, Master Sergeant Samuel Doe, helped lead a coup against the True Whig monopoly of power. He was not a descendant of the settlers, and was not well-educated in any formal sense. The hinterland was delighted. Anxious to master the instruments of the new government he came to dominate, and desperate to retain power after he had acquired it, he drew on an array of traditional beliefs, rituals and practices that ensured his survival as he set about a reign of incompetence, brutalities and a rigged election. Ten years later, when he was in turn overthrown by another coup, he had to be killed in a special way to neutralize his by now legendary personal powers. Even so, there were many who were sure that his corpse would be unable to rot.

What began now was the contest of 'traditional' powers. The most traditionally powerful, the one who drew his strength most from arcane cultural practices, would be seen to defeat all others. As Liberia plunged into chaos, competing militias – increasingly youthful – would partake in condensed rituals to bring power and invulnerability, to bring protection from the vengeful spirits of those whom they had brutally and casually killed. One of the most tragic and visual evidences of the rush to extrapolate from tradition, in a time of compressed stress, was the wearing of masks and costumes by the fighters. These were meant to cover them in protective auras. The swiftness of their ritual initiations, the scarcity of traditional mask makers, and the syncretic and hybrid nature of by now all existence in Liberia, saw the teenage fighters taking to the field dressed as Mickey Mouse, characters from Mad Max, or cross-dressed in wigs like Beyonce. The advent of Charles Taylor as a warlord who would become president saw also the rumours of his power having been gained by rituals of cannibalism. In a way Taylor tried extraordinarily hard to demonstrate to the hinterland that he was not one of the *congos*, the descendants of the free-slave settlers, at least in his thought and habits – despite a US college education. Taylor was also extremely hungry for power and, his urbane Massachusetts demeanour and New England syllables notwithstanding, immersed himself in hinterland rituals and *poro* practices. The saying '*poro* business is eating business' led to the widespread belief that Taylor had ritualistically eaten much human flesh. As Stephen Ellis said, in his outstanding account of the Liberian civil war of 1989–97, there is no actual evidence Taylor did this. However, the traditional, sometimes years' long *poro* rite of initiation into adulthood certainly utilized the *metaphor* of consumption. In the cruder, compressed times of civil emergency and war, it is thought that the rites also became compressed and cruder, and there is the possibility that metaphor was taken as something literal. There are indeed many accounts of cannibalism among other atrocities. Whether real, or as a macabre tale for a low public relations, Taylor seemed to revel in the legend of his *poro*-induced powers. He won the 1997 elections, pretty much on the premise that it was better to vote for him than be killed by him. His presidency did nothing to end violence; the spillover to Sierra Leone saw similar historical bifurcations flare up into huge brutalities; the fight for control of diamond mines added to the conflicts, and dampened Western enthusiasm to intervene – war diamonds were, after all, cheaper to obtain and made a larger retail profit than any 'legitimate' stones.

In the end, the other states of West Africa were instrumental in plucking Taylor into exile. The diplomacy was excruciatingly slow and polite, but it was clear he had become a gross embarrassment to all around. Perhaps others feared their own 'mongrels under the board'. Certainly Taylor was *understood*, while loathed. But he had transgressed the sense of *proportion* that is the governing politesse in much of Africa between what may be traditional practice and what seeks, all the same, to develop as a form of modernity.

The cohabitation of the arcane and modern

Donal Cruise O'Brien has written how, in Senegal, the three Islamic Sufi Brotherhoods have played an important role as an intermediary between government and people. It is a constantly renegotiated role but, precisely because urban and governmental Senegal is so Francophile, the goodwill of the Sufi leaders in the rural areas – which are not – is essential. Islam, however, is an established religion and the Sufi variant has strong traditions and hundreds of years of written poetry and philosophy that have inflected the theological content of Sufi belief. The lack of negotiability and proportion between government and religion comes with newly syncretic beliefs – often charismatic and founded on a single recent 'prophet'. Often seemingly bizarre and beyond rational interpretation, the mixture of animism, extrapolated other local spiritualities, and usually Christianity provide an explosive mixture when linked with ethnic lobbies or uprisings. It does not even have to be syncretic, but the case in Rwanda of Roman Catholic

111

bishops urging on the slaughter of the Tutsis, and blessing it, spiritually validating it, is rare. It is more often as was the case in Uganda, where in 1986 Alice Lakwena rose up as head of an Acholi rebellion and founded the Holy Spirit army with a *mélange* of beliefs. Heike Behrend has written about this in a most sympathetic way. After the military defeat of Alice – but the new government of Museveni, who is still Ugandan president, just squeaked it – the remnants of her forces and others hostile to a regime not dominated by the Acholis have waged a civil war in the peripheries of the country that has lasted till this day. They conduct atrocities, kidnap children, and keep fighting in the name of the Lord. Museveni does not negotiate with them, so the conflict continues. When, in my second appendix, I retell in fictional style the story of Alice, it is not to endorse what came behind her, but to give a flavour of how complex syncretic beliefs can be – and how much like our own purportedly more 'structured' beliefs they are. Behrend stresses that Alice was not a witch. Indeed, she cast out witches in the land of the Acholis, acting as a Christian exorcist. I have, however, called her a witch in my retelling and, in doing so, follow Chabal and Daloz in their controversial book, *Africa Works*, in which they argue that informal procedures, a 'social rationality', namely something that makes sense to those involved even if it does not to those who are not, patronage networks, and witchcraft are all viable and even necessary instruments of 'administration' against the background of vacuous and weak states. In that sense there is no primitivism implied in calling someone a 'witch'.

Stephen Ellis and Gerrie ter Haar have written about the importance of religion in African politics, particularly new and revivalist religions. Charismatic faiths are a natural development of Pentecostalism – the making of the spirit world material in the form of worship, possession, and power. Just as Charles Taylor sought to make himself powerful by rituals in Liberia, so too the mark of being 'chosen' in the biblical sense is a powerful endorsement of any ambitious politician. The privileged access to the secret world of God also gives the aura of being special, unable to be defeated, of knowing something others do not. Vote for me because God has already voted for me. Insofar as there is a scriptural base, such demeanours are negotiating tools; in other words, the recipients of God's grace cannot claim more than what the Bible allows anyone; they can claim they have it in special abundance and should therefore be supported. Where the political figure draws from a variety of beliefs and selects among them, only his personal theology arbitrates those beliefs. Weberian charisma can then be seen in religion as much as politics, or in religion as a pathway to politics.

Returning to Kaunda, the use of solemn Christianity sat well on him for some years. He exploited a pacificism that was Christian – turning the other cheek – and Ghandian when he had no military means to resist Rhodesian and South African incursions in the 1970s and early 1980s. The piety wore thin as time wore on. Nevertheless, new brands of charismatic, and hypocritical, piety are now part of Zambian politics. Roy Clarke's satire of *Never Mumbo Jumbo* is a direct reference to Nevers Mumba, the pastor who became a vice-president. The blend of politics and religion is something long unseen in the West, but it would be like one of the stadium-filling US evangelical preachers – all singing, hand-clapping, amen-ing, positive-platitudinizing and tithe-wringing – becoming secretary of state. Insofar as only the Bible is used as their foundation, their messages contain some predictability. It is the syncretic religiosity of the charismatics outside government, but longing to overthrow it, that is harder to understand and mediate.

The Commission's view of culture

The Commission for Africa went out of its way quite early in its report to emphasize the need to respect African cultural values. The report rejects any view of a static culture, no matter how conceived. New technologies, 'the mobile phone in particular' are 'having a profound cultural impact' (Chapter 3.3 para. 18), and this is certainly the case. If Alice Lakwena had come a little later, she would have organized her uprising with mobile phones. The statement about new technologies means nothing in itself. It was what the technologies are used for that counts.

The report does acknowledge the diversity of Africa, and hence its cultures (3.4.2); the huge array of invisible networks (3.4.3); and religious networks (3.4.4). But its entire stress is on how to understand culture to facilitate development. 'A cultural urgency underpins our findings across this report and cultural dimensions form part of the argument for the actions we propose' (3.6 para. 50). In fact, cultural dimensions are far from apparent in most of the later report. Chapter 3 is a genuflection, a 'hoping for the best' in a situation where understanding and empathy are difficult for Western policy-makers. The understanding of culture is not something with an instrumental outcome and, in the case of development, Chabal and Daloz make some trenchant comments.

They are sceptical of the emphasis on democracy for, in a protracted condition of national economic woe, what is there that an opposition party can promise? There are seldom alternative platforms that differ radically from the government's or any other party's. There may be promises of greater honesty and transparency, but there are very few political figures in Africa, in or out of office, who come without corrupt baggage – and the voters know that. Very often it comes down to personality politics, or the bandwagons of interest groups. If the former, then the spectacle in today's Zambia, where the papers are daily full of splinter parties and their 'presidents' insulting one another, is as instructive as it is distressing. It is sometimes possible to read the political news for days without encountering an actual discussion about policy. If the latter, the bandwagons of interest groups, then the individual citizen is marginalized. In all this, it is no wonder that people turn to beliefs, new religions and new mythologies compounded from the 'best' of the old, that are at odds with the political establishment. In those terms, the carnage in Liberia may be seen not only as the lust for power of Charles Taylor but as the awful unleashing of cultural forces – however condensed and bastardized – to destroy all that a failed system of formal government imposed upon the nation.

Chapter 8

Coming through shit: the lone trek of the citizen towards the future

Ayi Kwei Armah's *The Beautyful Ones Are Not Yet Born* remains one of Africa's greatest novels. It is the account of a person's struggle to be honest, literally in the face of shit. The sheer coprophagic intensity of the book is overwhelming – yet the protagonist emerges as almost a luminous figure. Not everyone considers it his greatest novel – or even a great novel at all. The Nigerian Nobel Prize-winner, Wole Soyinka, thought it a poor work. But there are few examples of existential morality in African literature. Morality is usually transacted through a group. I do not want to enter the generalizing debate about whether Africans are more communal than others. How can you tell? Both the Kantian and Arab laws of hospitality are acute, and bespeak a communitarianism that nevertheless does not deny individualism. In this final chapter I want to focus on what the individual African citizen faces. In many ways the array of complexities and ambiguities he or she faces makes for the most benighted, but also the most heroic citizen on earth. I want to elaborate a little my final chapter in an earlier small book, *Composing Africa*, and here I had better confess that I am inching my way to some form of articulation of Africa that defies a single attempt. The present effort may be (it is hoped) better than the last. The next may be less imperfect again. Or perhaps the efforts are all hopeless. One thing for sure, the citizen of Africa cannot afford hopelessness, although his or her condition would crush those who sought a brief solidarity in the G8 concert in Hyde Park.

This is perhaps to be harsh. One has a solidarity based on one's own experience. Even in Zimbabwe, until recently, it was possible to visit as a hermetically-sealed tourist. Then the taxis and coaches had petrol to take tourists to the sights, and the value of the local dollar would of course allow munificent purchases for the return home. This sort of experience is still possible in many parts of Kenya, in Gambia, guarded resorts in Mozambique. Getting off the beaten track means more than a game park with a hotel in the trees. The Latin American novelist, Gabriel García Márquez, once said in a chance aside that the periphery will know the metropole very well, almost intimately from its daily reception of images, news and fashions; but the metropole would know the periphery not at all.

Latin America at least has had more time to fashion a consciousness of itself – and then broadcast it to an astounded West. The magical realism of its novels, Marquez's being a case in point, rely not on a pre-reality but on a hyper-reality, a reality not under control. Something that is solid is made fluid. The problem for Africa is first to find what is solid. There has not been a great magically realist novel from Africa. Nor has there been the sort of epic family drama of Brazil, where rival families struggle and murder one another over ownership of land. Nothing in Africa is comparable to Jorge Amado's *The Violent Land* in this respect – simply because the issue of land has not yet been sufficiently settled for private families to fight over it. The Mugabe entry point to this issue is belated and disastrous, but really is a later starter than it should have been. And I would have liked to see emerge from Africa something like Mario Vargas Llosa's *The War of the End of the World*, where religion and dispossession confront politics in armed uprising. Someone needs to write the Alice Lakwena story in this manner, and perhaps I am trying to labour that point in my appendix. The personnel in African novels are small clusters, as in Ngugi's *Petals of Blood*. Kwei Armah's moral existentialism is, as I said, an exception. But I want to use the motif of aloneness, because it may be the best entry point to an appreciation of what confronts Africa – by taking it right down, in terms of what I have written in this short book, to the lone individual.

The settled

I use this term, 'settled', to indicate what my hypothetical individual citizen faces in 'normal' life. It is a composite individual of course, but he or she faces some ten sites of transaction as a process of settled normality. I refer to them loosely as sectors. If he or she transgresses any of these sectors, he or she must build support and safeguards from others.

1. The national political impact upon his or her life.
2. The local political and administrative impact upon his or her life.

3. The impact of political party organization, both nationally but, importantly, locally upon his or her life.

These are three 'political sectors' from which there is often no escape. In terms of the third, party politics, this was unavoidable in the days of single-party states. You signed up and were seen to do so, or you were accused of disloyalty. In the new days of 'democracy', wearing an opposition party T-shirt is an invitation to being beaten up by the militants of Robert Mugabe's party. Accosted by a militant, pleas of party neutrality are as dangerous as declared membership of the 'other side'.

4. The impact of formal economy upon his or her life.
5. This impact carries the possibility of encounters and trans-actions with the international political economy – aid workers, development consultants, and all their apparatus.
6. The impact of the informal economy upon his or her life.

These are three 'economic sectors', to which should perhaps be added a sector of corruption and corrupt practice, but I would normally include those as facilitators of the patronage networks to which I refer below. None of this is to mention a further sector of mere subsistence, the eking of survival, but I include that as an extreme of informal economy.

The demands and impacts of politics and economy, their various institutions and powerful personnel, can be such that resistance becomes located in beliefs from earlier times. They may be *restated*. After all, originally, these beliefs did not have to confront modernity. Now they are used to confront modernity's failure as far as our citizen is concerned. The sectors and institutions of modernity have not served him or her well.

7. The impact of ethnic identity and organization upon his or her life.
8. The impact of magical or spiritual beliefs and practices to provide a protection and protagonizing force found nowhere else.
9. The subscription to – not just the impact from – patron–client relationships, even at the end of the patronage chain. Some access to some form of power and support is better than none at all. These relationships may have an ethnic character, or a religious one.

And, finally, there is:

10. The impact of crime and social violence upon his or her life.

If this is normality, then the *perils of normality* are manifold but, with ingenuity and habituation, negotiable. And that is what the citizen of Africa does. He or she daily negotiates all these sectors of pressure and duress. But these are settled sectors, that is they account for normality, for stability. They demand a settled decophrenia perhaps, but they are all nego-tiable and transactable. This does not mean they are necessarily predictable, rational, fair or easy. The citizen has become, by all this, the most sophisticated of creatures. Given that the state is still developing, he or she must carry all its omissions and abuses. On top of that, however, he or she must often bear the unsettled.

The unsettled

In conditions of 'unsettlement' society can no longer be 'civil', neither in an etymological nor technical sense. These are periods of upheaval, such as war, coups, the immediate aftermath of coups, and the atrocious rule of warlords or politicians or 'liberation' groups who deliberately terrorize, kill and maim all they choose or 'pick'. There were periods in Amin's Uganda, and in Somalia, that fit this last condition. This much does not need elaboration. There is, however, a third body of conditions.

The shaken

I borrow this term from the Czech philosopher much admired by Vaclav Havel, Jan Patocka. He wrote of the mêlée, when two armies charge at each other and intersect. Men on both sides are all mixed up. They do not know who they are fighting, but they have to fight desperately to survive. Many fight with true belief in a cause and great courage – but all of them are equal at that moment as all face death. This is his metaphor for when society is a maelstrom of inescapable violence and, whatever the original competing rationalities, that moment of mêlée is a moment where thought and compassion are no more. At that moment all are swept along and it is kill or be killed. I wonder whether the Liberias and Rwandas of Africa fit into the 'shaken', into the condition of terror.

***

The great problem with the Commission for Africa was the same problem with the G8. They spoke to governments. Their

121

recommendations were to do with official policies. And the membership of the Commission was largely governmental or official – Geldof being an exception. In the report's cover photograph he is the one with the longest hair among the men and the only one not wearing a tie. He knows how to wear one. He turned up for Elton John's 2005 birthday wearing white tie, tails and his state medals. Seated second right in the photo is Meles Zenawi, the prime minister of Ethiopia. Insofar as his forces, together with those of the Eritreans, overthrew the dictatorship of Mengistu, he was a breath of fresh air in Ethiopia. The advent of war between the two former allies led to terrible casualties on the Eritrean front, but it was a war broadly supported in Ethiopia. Meles Zenawi called elections in 2005 and they were robustly contested and, largely, peacefully held. But when it was clear from reports of the count that Zenawi was going to win – but not by as much as he had hoped – he showed his teeth to the opposition, refused to release the final results, and his security forces killed a large number of people protesting his refusal. It was a disaster for his democratic credentials – but the Commission photograph was taken before the killing in cold blood of his own citizens, and he is shown sitting beside Hilary Benn, Britain's overseas development minister. Official Africa has a long way to go before its commitment to fairness and transparency is more than merely tentative. Speaking as officials and ministers to other officials and ministers bypasses the Africa of ordinary Africans.

The report mentions the need for increased work with and through non-governmental organizations but, again, this does not necessarily bring assistance closer to its beneficiaries. NGO aid protocol and procedures are exactly the same as those for official aid. Indeed, NGO activity can be as intrusive as it is helpful in the lives of small communities. All manner of preformed agendas and 'off the peg' projects are marshalled and 'donated' – whether they are truly needed or not. Partha Dasgupta recounts a revealing story. It is set in India but may as well have been set in Africa. A certain village was located miles from water. Every day the women had to walk those miles, fill their pots with water, then carry the water on their heads back to the village. The intervening NGO was sure at first sight what was needed – a well inside the village. Accordingly, a well was dug and water was made available without any need for walking. All that labour by the women would no longer be required. The women hated it. The three hours it used to take to travel to the stream, pot the water, and carry it home had been hours of freedom and womanly association, had been hours of sisterhood. Now it was not a case of three hours saved from labour. Their husbands just invented new things for them to do, and all that daily refreshment of female solidarity had been taken from them. It is amazing that, in this day of gender awareness, no one had bothered to ask the women if they wanted a well. It was just obvious that one was needed, wasn't it? And well-digging was probably on the list of projects given approval by the NGO's auditors and governors. It probably even had a quota of wells it had to dig in any one year. The NGOization of Africa – they are everywhere – has not done any better than official aid projects. There are of course conspicuous exceptions, and local people have learnt to play one NGO off against another and get what they actually want. But there is a litany of failed projects that is extensive and several that might best be described as 'well-meaning'.

Three scenarios

What should be done? Here are three different scenarios. None is perfect. Number One: cancel all debt without any conditions; liberalize trade; end all aid except for emergencies; then just let them get on with it. If it sinks, it will be their fault; if it floats, it will be their accomplishment. Less harshly, the ending of all debt and trade restrictions would at least give politicians, in government and opposition, some prospect of resources and liquidity over which to argue. They might have to embrace their electorates with real policies, and this would be the making of actual democracy, namely providing a choice, not just of personnel and party label, but of actual governmental intentions. *This will not occur, since the starting point involves the ending of aid. An entire Western 'industry' will go out of business, compassion must find other outlets and, frankly, hospitals and schools will require assistance – almost certainly from the outside – for some time to come.*

Number Two: give aid only to entrepreneurs. Develop the informal sector so that much of it can start graduating to the formal sector. Allow a crossover. For a time there will be ventures that have a foot in both camps. This will enable the growth of new sites of income. Businesses will be seen to work and the need for small-time corruptions and brown-nosing rich and powerful patrons will diminish. More importantly, the growth of a new entrepreneurial class will create a middle ground, a site of mediation, between the powerful and corruptly rich on the one hand, and the benighted poor on the other. It will allow society to develop an actual economic pluralism, and this might be much more important than the imposition of Westminster-style political pluralisms. *This will not occur, as no auditor of any governmental expenditure in the*

West will sanction investment in an informal, unregulated, initially 'outlaw' enterprise.

Number Three: if it all must be much as it is (and it will be; in this sense the report of the Commission for Africa will be very successful; the current paradigm will be slightly liberalized but will remain), then work even harder to lift trade restrictions. Why they are there seems a mystery. As noted above, total sub-Saharan African trade is only 2 per cent of the world total – of which South Africa contributes half, that is the rest of sub-Saharan Africa manages 1 per cent. This will not for any time soon grow enough to threaten anyone. *All* of sub-Saharan Africa might one day threaten Belgium – but even that day is not near. The trade restrictions are there not because of a threat from Africa, but because lifting them might be seen as a precedent for lifting those against economies elsewhere that really could compete and, in some sectors, even overwhelm the current advantage of the West. The special case of Africa might raise the hackles of for example the Chinese, desperate to expand their markets. The Chinese even cultivate Zimbabwe as a market, or at least as a market entry point to the rest of southern Africa. The deluded Robert Mugabe imagines they are coming to his country to help Zimbabwe. But Africa must be treated as a special case if it is, even slowly, to be able to grow out of poverty.

Back to music, back to Eden

When Geldof conceived his G8 concert in Hyde Park and other locations around the world, he contacted all his musician friends and twisted their arms to play for free. It became plainly clear he had no black African musician friends. In Hyde Park the cast was painfully white. Birhan Weldu's tear-inducing appearance was a contrast to almost everyone else who commanded a microphone that day. Black Americans played on the other side of the Atlantic, but actual black Africans were invited to Britain as an afterthought to play at Cornwall's Eden Project, and that only because of Peter Gabriel's intervention and list of contacts. The Eden Project, within Buckminster Fuller geodesic domes, aims to house all the world's botanical variety. At least that day a motley audience heard some of the variety of Africa's musicians. Even then, the television broadcasts, cutting from one concert location to another, gave very little coverage to Eden. Perhaps the music was too complex? The performers not household names? It all seemed a gross oversight, which even technology did not try to remedy.

There are of course African musicians who are very well-known in the West: Orchestra Baobab from Senegal, Youssou N'Dour again from Senegal, Salif Keita from Mali, Ladysmith Black Mambazo from South Africa, King (he really is a king) Sunny Ade from Nigeria, Ali Farka Touré from Mali, Hugh Masekela and Miriam Makeba from South Africa. The Francophonic West African musicians in that list, such as N'Dour, clearly have Islamic influences. N'Dour is very open about his Sufiism. They are multicultural ambassadors in more ways than one. It is not just that Africa needs to do more fusion with the West and the values of equality and transparency; it is also that the West needs to fuse more with Africa – and discover a disparate continent already well versed in the arts of fusion. Both N'Dour and Sunny Ade have released more than 100 albums, mostly for local consumption, so even the most avid Western fan is ignorant of most of their repertoire. But it means that much of Africa finds entertainment, release and understanding in music. In Zimbabwe, musicians such as Oliver Mutukudzi and Thomas Mapfumo are so popular, they can record songs that are inflected but, all the same, clearly critical of the government and Mugabe's hard men will not 'pick' them. The G8 concerts had a chance to pick up on Africa speaking for itself, and blew it.

I retain an admiration for Bob Geldof. In a way he has made an easy target because he tried to do so much. But at least he tried. He began life as a rock star. No one would have thought he had a future as a conscience of the world. His problem was that he thought he might use Tony Blair, but Blair is a master and who used whom is clear enough. But Geldof's generation has done so much more and brought much greater global understanding than any earlier generation of popular musicians. I am less hard on Geldof than George Monbiot (*Guardian*, 6 September 2005), but share Monbiot's dismay that, after all the G8 posturing, many of the Western financial pledges will not be honoured, and the much touted sums set aside for aid and debt relief draw in fact from the same limited pot. George Harrison began both the charity concert and inter-cultural fusion for the young. Geldof is really his only successor, even if he has to work on the fusion – and lose his sense of grandeur in being an associate of the powerful.

Is there a future for Africa? The original Eden, that is the location of humanity's first ancestors, was in Africa. Out of Africa was from where we all came – squabbling, multitudinous, unreasonable, conspicuously consuming, consumptive and sick, world war mongers twice in one century, tyrannical, ethnic cleansers as in Bosnia, committers of genocide as in the Nazi death camps, mass killers of the innocent as in both Hiroshima and New York on 9/11, militarily dictatorial as in Spain, Portugal, Greece, Brazil and Argentina until very recently, and followers after charismatic holy-men as in Waco, Texas or Jonestown, Guyana. Humanity's list is not a pretty one. What redeems it is not just the huge reservoirs of goodness and generosity, but the very complexities and ambiguities that go into being both evil and good. Maybe we ate from the wrong tree; maybe not. But the ambiguities of Africa parallel our own. And we did play a role in ensuring that Africa entered the twentieth century both late and from a lower base than all of ours. Africa has not always helped itself, it has often tortured itself, but we should perhaps make more time for it, more effort and, yes, a special case for it. The new millennium should not see such a disparity between one continent and the rest of humanity. But we should not expect it to be easy. Understanding Africa is not easy. And we should not think any people is pure and beyond ambiguity.

Appendix One
Endless *chimurenga*: the war without end in Zimbabwe

U DI – the Unilateral Declaration of Independence of Ian Smith's white Rhodesia in 1965 – was not only a moment of crisis and decision on the part of the black nationalist parties, and on the part of surrounding states that had, like Zambia in 1964, just come to independence based on majority rule, it was a moment of crisis and indecision for the British government. The Britain of the 1960s was not only the crucible of youth culture – the Beatles in Liverpool, the Rolling Stones in Richmond – it was an economically stretched state. Britain had to seek loans from the IMF, the currency lost value, the Harold Wilson government tacked into every buffeting wind and lost a swathe of its Labour values. Not only that, but Britain's sense of international relations had also diminished; the withdrawal from east of Suez after 1956 was a huge blow to its self-esteem and it, frankly, had no appetite for military confrontation. When UDI came in 1965, the British military leaders were extraordinarily pessimistic about the possibility of putting down the rebellion, and cautioned it could only be done at great expense and risk to lives. Wilson temporized, then embarked on a policy of negotiations and sanctions, but had underestimated the obstinacy of the Smith regime.

The policy of bringing UDI to heel through attrition was not well-received by the Commonwealth, itself grouped around an independent Commonwealth Secretariat for the first time in 1965. The Commonwealth summit of 1966, held in Lagos, was a fraught affair. Protracted sessions saw secretaries fainting in their typing pools as Wilson pleaded the imminence of UDI's end. If nothing else, the issue established the direction of Commonwealth relations to this day: Africa, especially southern Africa, would be the main theme; and debate would centre on British action and inaction.

Within Rhodesia itself, the white minority government was indeed a minority. It was likened to all of Britain being ruled only by the inhabitants of Brighton. The colonial system of administration was maintained and, even by the beginning of 1980, when majority rule finally came, there was still a system of provincial commissioners and district commissioners. The civilian administration was mirrored by a military machine that was divided into joint operational commands and sub-joint operational commands. When civil war finally began, the Rhodesian forces had geographical spread, rapid reinforcements from its joint operational commands and sub-joint operational commands, and mechanized technology – warplanes, helicopters, improvised armoured cars with Browning machine guns, and heavier side-arm ordinance than that used by the guerrillas.

To an extent that has been under appreciated, that military disposition greatly influenced guerrilla strategy. It had to be mobile and evasive; it had to avoid sites of Rhodesian force concentration; it had to have escape routes; and guerrilla columns could never be weighed down by provisions or heavy arms. It also meant much experimentation as, frankly, quite raw guerrilla units would be sent out – cannon fodder is what we would call it – to test the response time of Rhodesian units. To keep morale and political consciousness high, commissar officers were as important as field commanders. The guerrillas took an awful beating in the early conflict that began with the Battle of Sinoia in 1966. It was the ZANLA (Zimbabwe African National Liberation Army) forces of what became Robert Mugabe's ZANU (Zimbabwe African National Union) party that undertook most of the fighting, although it should be said that the ZIPRA (Zimbabwe People's Revolutionary Army) of Joshua Nkomo's ZAPU (Zimbabwe African People's Union) played an important role in tying down Rhodesian forces; in other words these forces could not be sent as reinforcements to the east, where ZANLA troops began to operate from the border at the end of 1972 and in earnest from 1976, shortly after the independence of Mozambique. Chinese training of ZANLA cadres and officers meant a clear Maoist battle strategy evolved. The soft targeting of civilian installations and farms, the merging with the local population, the exemplary executions, and the spy network within ZANLA to stifle dissidence all had a Chinese liberation war prototype. The use of Chinese AK-47s also dictated battlefield doctrine. These are light weapons that not only utilize the typical AK spray action but, because very light, are hard to aim accurately. For years the guerrillas were ill-famed for firing high, unable to control kickback from their weapons. But their lightness meant ease of carrying in the field, and their simplicity meant ease of maintenance and cleaning, and reliability. They were, however, of little use against armoured cars and helicopters, and even in fire fights with more heavily armed Rhodesian troops. From the beginning, guerrilla doctrine accepted huge casualties.

What all this field engagement and painful learning of military lessons meant, however, was that diplomacy became increasingly marginalized. Sacrifices were being made, atrocities were being committed on both sides, and there was blood and conscience for which to answer. The Smith and Home constitutional proposals were voted down by African voters in 1972. Kenneth Kaunda's summit with South African Prime Minister Vorster, on the Knife Edge Bridge beside Victoria Falls in 1975, provided no solutions. The Kissinger plan of 1976 made little progress (although its acceptance of land as a key issue would return to haunt the twenty-first century), as did the Geneva talks of 1976 and the Anglo-American initiative of 1977–78. The internal settlement between Ian Smith and Abel Muzorewa of 1979 was far too little too late. By that stage it is fair to say that the guerrilla forces, despite much trumpeting of its 'liberated areas', were at least denying the Rhodesian army ease of access and ease of control over much of the northeast, and there was contestation in many areas. Such control as the Rhodesians maintained came at great cost, and it was clear that, even if the guerrillas were still far from winning the war, the Rhodesians certainly could not win it at all. South African political and economic support would not extend to significant military support – for the South African reading of the situation was that a guerrilla victory was indeed, in the medium-term future, possible; and it did not want an antagonistic fully militarized and victorious black government on its doorstep. If there had to be a black majority government, it had to be somehow civilianized, and South African pressure on Smith and Muzorewa to attend the Lancaster House talks at the end of 1979 was considerable.

Guerrilla strategy, because weak militarily, had to adopt sufficient popular and cultural emblems to ensure safe passage, provisioning, and protection from rural villages. These villages had to become like mini sub-joint operational commands to parallel, several levels down, the Rhodesian capacity to re-equip and reinforce itself from bases of local operation. This is not to say, in the popular anthropological parlance, that the guerrilla forces 'invented' or 'reinvented' or 'imagined' traditions to which they could affiliate themselves. They almost certainly *manipulated* aspects of spiritual tradition, not to mention the spirit mediums who were its guardians and interlocuteurs. Nor is it true to say that all guerrillas were fighting for a nationalism that was also culturally authentic. The present author met many in the assembly points of the 1980 cease-fire who had gone to war for precisely those almost abstract Enlightenment values of freedom and equality – and, in conversations with him, they marginalized the spiritual and national importance of land. Having said that, it must be immediately counterpointed by the importance of spiritual tradition *as something of authentic importance to many fighters, as something of* authenticating *importance to commanders needing to motivate their troops, and as a doctrine of* nationalist authenticity *to political leaders.* Insofar as spiritual tradition relied upon a spirit world intimate with the same land upon which humans trod, and insofar as land and nation make easy conceptual bedfellows, there came into being a crossover philosophy of liberation that was simultaneously traditional and socialist-modern. The linking motif was not that there were spirits of the land, but that land was evidently *material*

133

and, as such, could be accommodated within both spiritual belief as a base for the spirits, and ideological formulations of a material base for revolution. Once the crossover was established its component parts could merge more fluidly, as I shall propose below.

To that extent, the famous debate between Ranger and Kriger has to be tilted in favour of Ranger. It is all very well to say that there were a range of factors – some certainly local and fractious – partaking of both the spiritual and material, that motivated, sustained and propagated armed struggle; but I am suggesting that, in the Zimbabwe case, it is possible to see the spiritual as the key animation of much else. It is the ghosts of *chimurenga*s past, after all, that are invoked in Mugabe's nationalization of land today. The spirit world has moved on. Now it is not the Nehandas of that world but the Border Gezis and Moven Mahachis. Despite a new generation of spirits, as it were, the *methodology* of thought and its linkages between spiritual precedence and material authenticity, between spiritual authentication and material ownership, are the same.

In the case of Gezi and Mahachi, their inscription 'into heaven' is Mugabe's, in his collection of speeches, *Inside the Third Chimurenga*. This is a book to which I wish to return. The antecedent literary work that populated heaven, or the spirit world, with new archetypes was Alexander Kanengoni's great novel, *Echoing Silences*, in which Herbert Chitepo and Jason Moyo among others address the great spirit convention of the skies, and to which are drawn all the casualties of the second *chimurenga*, the war of liberation that ended in 1980. Although Kanengoni's book lamented the failure of revolution's honesty after 1980, it established lineage in the spirit world. Mugabe has added to that lineage and conceives of himself as re-establishing the revolution in all its honesty, shrugging off the hindrances of international expectation (including South African expectation), and devoting everything to the national authentication of *his* revolution, and himself. To spiritual tradition and material ideology there is now added a certain personalization not only of rule, but of history and destiny, and all of this has achieved a holistic fluidity that makes Mugabe, not so much hard to interpret, but hard to predict and *measure*.

****

The first *chimurenga* occurred in 1896, when a huge uprising of both Shona and Ndebele dissidents killed 400 settlers. The white response was considerably more brutal than anything the uprising accomplished, and began a process of consolidating formal ownership of land in favour of the white settlers. This was completed in 1923, when the constitution entrenched 'native reserves' and, in 1930, when the Land Apportionment Act divided Rhodesia between private white ownership and what were called 'tribal trustlands'. The best and most land went to the settlers. This meant the beginning of a modern history, first of defeat for the black Africans, and then of legalized appropriation. The uprising, however, had clear spiritual as well as political animation, and the redemption of defeat by victory in the second *chimurenga*, the war of independence, also drew from spiritual as well as political sources. The redemption of appropriation, however, the recapture of land, did not accompany independence.

At the Lancaster House talks in 1979, Lord Carrington, the British chairman, pointedly skirted the issue of land. The negotiations were torturous and fractious but, on 15 October, the Rhodesian delegation accepted the need for elections under British authority. This immediately allowed Carrington to impose a 'take it or leave it' ultimatum on the guerrilla delegation. Carrington did recognize he could not wish away the issue of land, but made the point that, after elections, a future government of Zimbabwe would want to widen the ownership of land. Mugabe admitted that he had been forced to give way, 'having to compromise on certain fundamental principles (meaning land), but only because there was a chance, in the future, to amend the position'. After Mugabe won the independence elections he again restated the need to reform land ownership. 'There must be fairness. Land must be shared.' Then he was speaking about sharing land in a way that was not arbitrary. 'We must abide by legality, but also by the requirement of fair play.' This fair play included compensation.

In the wake of the 1992 drought Mugabe sought again to prioritize land redistribution, and did so with the Land Acquisition Act of that year. The (largely white) commercial farming lobby – to international quarters such as the IMF – was largely successful in quieting this drum; but for a while Mugabe seemed adamant. 'Let us, you see, carry out this act once and for all. Those who support, support, those who will want to sabotage, let them sabotage. We will go through that path of comforts and discomforts and we will evolve measure ourselves in the process of remedying that.' The 'evolution' of measures suggested that there was as yet no operational plan. There never really has been and, such as there was, was dependent on the trickle of British funds to help finance it. Even so, the combination of drought – with limited food surplus being obtainable from the commercial farms – and the successful

Commonwealth summit in Harare in 1991 suggested to Mugabe both that his dues had been paid to the international community and that something should be done about land. The 'sunset' clauses in the constitution that came down from Lancaster House had set, and it was time to do something new. The need to accommodate IMF conditionality postponed what, rhetorically at least, Mugabe was signalling as inevitable.

By 1996 Mugabe's position had hardened in the face of British reluctance to help fund compensation. 'We are going to take the land and we are not going to pay for the soil. Our land was never bought (by the settlers), and there is no way we could buy back the land.' The point is that, from the very beginning, Mugabe has been consistent about the central issue of land. The only inconsistency has been over how to reappropriate it.

He has also been at pains to assert the continuous meaning of *chimurenga*. This has been within Terence Ranger's aptly coined phrase, the 'ownership of patriotic history'. Only those who liberated within the second *chimurenga* can draw validation from the first, as they set about the third. It is an ownership of validation, and of time. Although Ranger's phrase is descriptive, Mugabe himself has been 'owning' patriotic history since the inception of his rule. The *gukurahundi* or whirlwind of repression that swept through Matabeleland in the 1980s can be seen, in one sense at least, as a monopolization of interpretation and ownership of *chimurenga and* its fruits. The interesting thing is that, when it comes to patriotic history, it is a patriotism of the Zimbabwe that was created by colonial boundaries. It sweeps Matabeleland and the Ndebele people into it so that, at Joshua Nkomo's funeral in 1999, Mugabe's oration effectively sought to appropriate the great eastern leader into his own Zimbabwe. Only 'after my assuring him of effective protection' did Nkomo return from Botswana in 1987 to begin talks on the Unity Accord that ended the *gukurahundi* – and also ended Nkomo's party as a challenger for power. In the collection of Mugabe's speeches, *Inside the Third Chimurenga*, the genealogy of heroes is made apparent: Mbuya Nehanda from the first *chimurenga*, all those from the second who are buried outside Harare at Heroes Acre – including Nkomo – and Border Gezi and Moven Mahachi from the third. The last two, close comrades of Mugabe, died in separate car accidents in 2001. They had been co-architects and supporters of the farm invasions and their deaths shook Mugabe greatly. He was reported as wondering whether the deaths were pre-monitions that the spirit world rejected his actions, and the Harare rumour mill went so far as saying that, at dinner, he was setting an extra placing for the spirit of Josaiah Tongogara – the liberation general who had also died (suspiciously) in a car crash on the eve of independence.

Harare, as any habitué knows, is always awash with rumours. It is in some ways the most gossipy capital on earth. There is no way of knowing whether any are true. The tenor of these particular rumours, however, to do with Gezi, Mahachi and Tongogara, stress the importance of a spirit world that validates or withdraws validation. They are here as anecdote and suggestion. What is more evident is Mugabe's memory of history in terms of its colonial origin. In an interview on the twenty-fifth anniversary of independence he said, 'memories do pile up, but the most remote ones, especially those which saw us suffer and the times when we were under real bondage, under colonial rule, those can never fade away, they remain forever.' To the pile of other ingredients – history and authentication – may be added *hurt*, and it is clear that Mugabe today draws much hurt from the way he perceives Tony Blair as condescending to him, exiling him from the international mainstream, and ignoring him. The speeches and advertising in all the elections since 2000 give the impression that they were contests between Robert Mugabe and Tony Blair. There is a considerable personalization of politics in Zimbabwe, both in the primacy of Mugabe and in his conflict with Blair. In the same twenty-fifth anniversary interview Mugabe made the root of the problem explicit: it was that he perceived Blair both as a bully and racist – in both senses a throwback.

> [Blair] is a bully, and bullies are not known to change their ways until they get someone who can actually knock them into submission. The bully continues to be a bully. Blair wants to continue this headmaster type of attitude – you must submit, after all you are a black nigger. And we say, 'Come on, small as we are, we have that sense of pride which exudes all the time. We are African and we are proud to be African.'

Elsewhere, Mugabe talks of the need for an 'African personality and an African culture', and that the root of this is 'land, land, land … it was our main grievance during the struggle. We built our struggle virtually on that grievance.'

But, because that struggle and grievance is not so apparent to a younger generation, Mugabe uses the example of Mao's Cultural Revolution – which, in China's case, *made* sacrifice and history apparent.

***

The feeling that land and history are more important than a headmaster's hectoring is not an isolated feeling on Mugabe's part. Kenneth Kaunda both lamented the exit of Zimbabwe from the Commonwealth after the Abuja summit in December 2003, and the fact that Mugabe had been demonized. A year later, in November 2004, he published a more considered piece on the issue, prioritized land as a key African issue, but again said 'it is not fair to demonize President Robert Gabriel Mugabe. Tony Blair and the British government had to do their part. In this case, it is that part that was central to the finding of a solution. This was agreed at the independence conference of Zimbabwe in London.' There is a return here to Carrington's essential elision of the land question at Lancaster House in order to achieve a constitutional solution to the crisis. But it begs the question as why, after independence, Mugabe did not move more swiftly to give operational meaning to an issue he has, over 25 years of independence, consistently championed.

A smarting Thabo Mbeki, returning from the Abuja summit, feeling he had been outmanoeuvred by Blair over Zimbabwe's membership, promptly published one of his ANC newsletters and simultaneously defended the Zimbabwean land seizures as a measure of last resort – 'with everything having failed to restore the land to its original owners in a peaceful manner, a forcible process of land redistribution became inevitable' – and insisted on the idea of an African cultural and political personality that could authentically shape the African destiny. He cited Ngugi wa Thiongo's book, *Decolonizing the Mind*, as an example of pioneering thought towards authenticity – and also took a barely veiled swipe at Blair that prefigured the later Mugabe description of him as a headmasterly bully: '[we will never] abandon our dignity as human beings, turning ourselves into grateful and subservient recipients ... happy to submit to a dismissive, intolerant and rigid attitude.' Blair, in his 1997 over swiftness to repudiate any residual British financial involvement in Zimbabwean land acquisition, sowed the seeds of wrath. Even so, it speaks little for Mugabe that he was prepared to wait upon British help in this matter from 1980 to 1997. Blair has not judged the situation well but, frankly, land was not a political priority, was not an urgency, until the end of the 1990s. Having said that, the *sentiment* for land has always been there, and Blair's lack of appreciation for this must go down as a mark of extreme under-briefing or cultural arrogance.

In all the great Zimbabwean novels, whether the authors are seen as against Mugabe – Chenjerai Hove and Yvonne Vera – or for him – Alexander Kanengoni – the treatment of land is something that borrows from the world of spirits, primal ancestry and primal myth.

Having said all that, Mugabe has always been plain in suggesting he would wish to talk with a British government without Blair. International approval, like national validation – even through rigged elections – is important to him. He would perhaps *like* to be the headmaster's favourite, which he once was. But his speeches are also to do with democracy and freedom, with legal procedure and economic accomplishment. These also have never been absent in 25 years of his rhetoric and, sometimes, his actions. These form a tension with the cultural authentication of policy, which requires land. The former set of values never disappeared entirely – though it took such a battering as to be unrecognizable in 2005 – but the latter has become triumphant.

***

It is in this context that the third *chimurenga* is not simply a spin-doctoring or opportunistic name grab by Mugabe. His book of speeches, *Inside The Third Chimurenga*, containing public statements from 1997 to 2001, reveals a preoccupation with land. Its prefatory epigram, from an unnamed Zimbabwean poem, sets the tone:

> But this land, this; the spirits dwelling in it
> Will not yield to such casual intimidation
> Neither will it give out its rich sad secrets
> To half-hearted tokens of transparent love.

Mugabe must take some blame for inaction between the second and third *chimurenga*s and, after all, one cannot claim that one wishes to be authentically free and lament the fact that the British did not pay for someone else's freedom. But I do not think the British, after Carrington and his perhaps tactically necessary side-lining of land, really grasped what was at stake in such a clearly former-settler colony. Nowhere else did settlers fight so long and hard. Nowhere else did they defy Britain with UDI. And it is not as if they had no love for the land themselves. They were *very* in love with it. Shortly after independence I came across a fragment of settler poetry. The whole piece and the name of its author have long disappeared from my library. It went something like this:

> And this land with its sweep and vista
> Its fruit and its power
> Its sunrise to sunset standing strong
>
> Is where we also stand
> Right or wrong.

Once UDI was declared in 1965, the terms of war were set. There was no turning back – although there were to be post-ponements of key issues over which war was fought. Kissinger rightly perceived land as a central issue. Carrington, in the light of Thatcheresque impatience to his right, and Common-wealth and African pressure on his left, and a string of failed international efforts to 'sort' Rhodesia as reminders, took a bloody-minded approach to the Lancaster House talks.

I was sure that previous attempts had failed through attempt-ing overprecision too early, through framing complex plans of ultimate order instead of coaxing minds towards the resolution of the next practical, intermediate step in debate. Each step might be imperfect in logic, or even in principle, but it must be realistic.

I wonder whether Lord Carrington might today revise these thoughts from his 1988 memoirs. Hindsight is of course a luxury and even Kenneth Kaunda blessed the outcome of the Lancaster House talks. We look upon Mugabe's third *chimu-renga* as a desperately late and desperately-planned endgame to what began long ago. Mugabe might look upon it as the begin-ning of the new African authenticity, in which he is leading the way – and acknowledged by many African admirers through-out the continent as leading the way. It is a late gambit. But can you have an ultimate goal without complex, practical and intermediate steps that ensure that the freed nation is not a hungry one, that the grand vistas are not barren, and that persuade a clearly ambivalent spirit world to bless it all by sending rain?

Appendix Two
Alice who almost became the witch president of Uganda

Alice and her march on Kampala

When Alice marched on Kampala, her columns were ranged like Wellington's squares of men defying Napoleon at Waterloo, with the exception of, among other things, the dust – the mountainous clouds of dust – outside Jinja. And, of course, Alice's high command of marshalls, the number of them disputed but growing story by story, gnarled and wise, rode inside her head, packed in there after the wide spaces of heaven, and they were agitating her to get on with the assault. Take Jinja and the path to Kampala is flat and clear: we will burn the seven hills and party in the Speke Hotel.

Alice

Look at the things they write of me. As if I had no knowledge or care. But God works in strange ways. He hollows out a space in the heads of those He has chosen. This is how God inhabits you; and, if not He, those He sends. I learnt that, many long years ago, spirits filled the head of a young woman in France. Those were the days when men wore armour, and this young woman began wearing armour in order to lead the men. And the men accepted her, seeing armour on the outside and knowing she held spirits within. They rose against the English who had come to their country and the English fought back, said the woman was a witch and they burned her and watched her die in great pain.

We are gentler in this country, even in this time. They defeated me, and God told the spirits to leave me. I have still this space in my head and I have not filled it. I call it Holy Space and, if any of the spirits should choose one day to visit, he will find his home just as he left it – clean, uncluttered, untouched by any regret. He would feel welcomed, just as he was welcomed before; for God does not choose a reluctant host. Those who defeated me saw that the spirits had left me and they left me alone. You can see they did not burn me. I was not dragged to the seven hills to stand trial in the place I had hoped to rule.

I would have ruled wisely, for my spirits came from all over the world: one came from America and, from him, I would have known how to talk of science; I could have talked to learned men and women; one came from Europe and, from him, I would have known the manners of a good president: I could have sat with the leader of France and not embarrass him at his own table; one came from China and, from him, I was already learning the energy that flies from the body to crush enemies; if I had become president I would have been able to ban tanks and rockets, yet still defend the country; and one, of course, was from a neighbouring African country, for we must learn to be good neighbours in Africa, and not fight like in the old days – although, in those old days, it was often white men, and Arab men before them, who encouraged us to fight among ourselves, before some of us realized what was happening and we united, as best we could back then, to fight them. We could be more united now, not just within our lands, but all over the world, and this is what I, Alice Lakwena, would have propagated had I become president of Uganda, and my country would have been the new Rome of a peaceful world, and this world would have come to see me, and bring gifts for all my people.

When people come now to my market stall, buy my vegetables and cooking oil made from bananas, buy the beer I make myself, some know I once bestrode the fields of battle. They are too polite to mention this because, in the end, I was defeated. They are kind and do not wish to embarrass me. But I know they point me out to strangers, whisper behind their hands, that I am the very Alice of the legends. Others know nothing and bargain down my prices as if I were any other market trader. And some wish to forget me; they want to carry on the revolution, and I am a painful memory; I am the memory of defeat. If anyone comes to kill me now, it will be those alongside whom I fought. Then there are the foreign visitors: tourists of strange and ancient forms of knowledge. They come with notepads and tape recorders, lately with portable computers. And they do not believe I am Alice. I do not look like a mighty warrior. Then I know the spirits still look after me, for they throw invisibility over me, and those who come to steal knowledge pass right by my market stall, and I smile, for once I was a great commander but now I am a small one of the world, so small that the world is unable to see me. But you see how God works. Perhaps he toyed with the idea that a small one should be president, and walk among other presidents; and these presidents would have had to learn some small ways, even if only to show they had good manners; then they would have expected to meet all the wise men in my entourage, hoping to bypass me as soon as possible – but all the wise men would have been inside my own head, and the presidents would have had to learn the humility of being with one who was small and strange, but contained many forms of wisdom.

So I smile each day at my market stall. My friends and well-wishers think I am happy. No, not happy, for I think I would have been a good president – but satisfied that I gave myself to God's little experiment. Increasingly, that is how I see it. Perhaps, in the future, in other lands, someone will come with great command of many forms of great wisdom. Then I will know that God has perfected what he began with me. I called my army the Holy Spirit Army, for what we call the Holy Spirit may be one, or it may be many agents of God. They hollow out part of someone's head, furnish it as they wish. It is important each spirit has his own room in which to be himself, but they all come together in that front part of the brain, to see what the freeholder sees – as if they stood on a balcony and saw before them the plains of Uganda and the road from one city to another, and saw the Holy Spirit Army that answered their call and, out of courtesy, and because I was chosen, consulted me also, so that I, Alice, was confidant to God's Spirit and, together, we briefly plotted a new world and a new mixture of humanity.

For I was worldly enough to understand the need for mixture; that is why I was chosen. And I knew what was happening when God's knife of light entered my head. It goes

147

in flat, and cleanly, and feels like wind. Once inside, the wind blows clear the room it wants. Whether the light and wind were one and the same, whether the spirits rode the wind or were the wind, I do not know. Whether God assembled the spirits or whether He used the ones available, again I do not know. But I know that they do not set about making you a warrior and prophetess immediately. They let you think that their thoughts are yours. Only, after some days of being pleased with yourself, you say that you have never had such thoughts before; then you say to them that you know they are living and thinking in that room you made available. You know the room is there, you do not know exactly how they have furnished it, or exactly who they are. By this speech you are able to establish a dialogue with them and come to know them. You must also come to like them. You must seem one person for, after all, the caravan that is now you must – already you know the dialogue will lead to this – travel across much of Uganda and mobilize many around you, as if you were one figure around whom many could stand. This is what a general must do. You must let the fighters have a centre. You cannot fight with them from behind. Even now I do not know how the government's generals could lead from behind, sending their officers, their cousins, to whip the young men forward. When I went forward, that is when my Holy Spirit Army went forward. We were like that surge of wind and I was at its heart. As wind entered me, so I entered the wind of our attacks.

For I want you to know that the spirits never became Alice. I remained conscious that I was Alice and the spirits were who they were. We talked and came to agreements but, always, I was a clear figure talking within myself. When the spirits left, I had lost friends but nothing of myself. And when officers of previously defeated armies came to join me, thinking they might overawe and influence a possessed and demented woman, I replied to them with lucidity – and the spirits let me talk as Alice, although this Alice had been taught by them the ways of war. It was I who wrote a book on how the army should fight. One of the spirits told me that a great German general had written such a book, which soldiers still read this day, so I too thought to write a book – on how to fight, and why you must believe something in order to fight. However much the spirits taught me about war, it was I who knew the need for belief. You do not die for nothing. You are not policy's instrument. You are policy who fights. But, because you do not wish to die, you fight with precautions; so my book was also about precautions.

A certain Major Okello, who fled the defeat of Amin's army

When the Tanzanians came to overthrow Amin, we were confident. We had more tanks and more aircraft. Even so, we had been surprised that they came. I had been one of those who advised Amin not to antagonize the Tanzanians; but he said that Nyerere is a man of peace; he speaks peace because he is too weak to fight and his army is also weak. Amin said that we could wreak havoc on the Tanzanian border, even occupy their side of the borderlands, and they would not come. When they came, they came with speech. That was the first thing that overawed us. They had language like lords. It was Swahili like our Swahili, but we spoke it in a vernacular that had lost precision. They spoke it with exactitudes, with an additional tense, Indian Ocean Swahili – with the lyric roll of syllables like Arabic, and with the educated lilt of men from Dar es

Salaam. For, if we imagined Kampala to be a sort of Rome, set on seven hills, Dar came against us with the conceit of Constantinople, a Christian wind against our arrogance, and African education against our militarism. The second thing we noticed was their immense organization. Their army had requisitioned every truck in the nation for the invasion. Whoever was their quartermaster knew how to do it, to deploy these trucks I mean, and what to put inside them. When they needed shells, there were shells. When they needed food, there was food. And then we realized how much they looked down on us. They had Ugandan rebels fighting with them. They let them walk alongside their tanks, but never ride on them. And they did not deign to fight us hand to hand. When we stood, they patiently brought up artillery and tanks – even if it took days – then blasted us until we retreated. Never once did they send infantry against us. They did not even send the Ugandan rebels. Their role was simply to march alongside. The Tanzanians gave, you see, this great sense of superiority, moral superiority – Nyerere's people come to flush out Amin's – and they would not sacrifice even a dog-eared, grubby and illiterate partisan. It was the same rendition of Sandhurst training that Indians have taken to their home. Bring up the armour. Do it methodically and patiently. But do it, all the same, faster than the enemy. We could not organize as quickly as they. Amin wanted a fighting retreat, in order to regroup in the north. But, as I said, every time we stood, the road we barred was blasted clean. Amin had wanted to save his armour for the counter, so we stood as infantry against tanks, and our own tanks never came. Soon, our men would not stand, and I myself would not stand without men around me. But the new governments that came after the Tanzanians – Lule, Binaisa, Obote whom Amin had earlier overthrown, and the successors of Obote, and now Museveni – never said to us we could surrender with honour; never said to us there would be guarantees in our homelands; but set about changing the world to something we could no longer recognize – something in which we had no place. So, when Alice rose, we saw her as our means also of resistance and fighting back. We emerged from our guerilla enclaves and went to meet her. We were welcomed. She said she would call me a brigadier, but I, alas perhaps, still have the pride that comes from some small education in other lands, and I told my men to continue calling me major. I became major in Israel, at the time Amin was secretly pulled and pushed to side with either Israelis or Arabs, and much money entered Uganda. Amin played this well enough, and I was proud that a people who know how to fight, even if not for cause we recognize, would rank me major. This was enough for me, and I noted that Alice never called herself field marshall or anything grand and, for me, this was to fight back, and to fight my way back to a recognition of myself before I too broke and ran before the Tanzanians.

An aide to Okello

The thing about this fight is that it is absurd. The professional soldiers are barely more than hundreds, and the thousands that lead the line are charismatic – not uniformed but smeared in oil, not precise in their march but harmonious in their hymns and spells. Not all have rifles. The soldiers, in these harsh times, form the second wave. We use the charismatics as shield – although they cannot know that. We hope they will pierce the enemy line – we hope they will attack only the areas we indicate – and we will enter swiftly, launch a secondary attack from behind; and we will not pause to ruin the enemy, but push on with greatest speed to Kampala, sucking the charismatics behind us, and hope that Kampala has sent all its army to defend forward and, in the manner of all fallen cities, greet us like heroes. We need to be there first, in any case, to stop the charismatics from sacking the city. There must be, after all, something for us to govern, and the pogroms to come must be judicious. We must not, this time, appear as Amin appeared to the world – arbitrary and ludicrous. But the world probably sees this, if it sees this, as ludicrous in any case. An army of possessed villagers led by a witch is bearing down on what was once a jewel of East Africa. And what stands before us, barring our way? An army of boys and teenagers, the orphans Museveni collected and trained in the Mountains of the Moon. They say many of these boys were orphaned by Amin and, knowing Amin's soldiers face them now, will fight even without their older officers. These boys are battle hardened, but came to this only by being whipped forward by the lieutenants of Museveni, this small man who thinks he is a Caesar in Kampala. A possessed army led by a witch faces an army of boys defending Rome, and who were themselves given the magic light of those distant mountains – mountains I myself have never seen. But those who see them, who journey in them, are said never to be the same again.

That much is hearsay and legend. What I know, at this moment, as a soldier, is that the enemy is used to victories but has never faced our numbers. They are used to going forward, but have little experience in defence. And, this time, there are no Tanzanian tanks. They have aircraft, but we are sure they have no reliable pilots.

Okello goes back and forth, from our tents to Alice Lakwena's, persuading the witch – the prophetess – to agree our plan. She cannot send the charismatics forward in a wave. They must aim for the weak spots in the enemy deployment. I feel for Okello. He led the stand against the Tanzanians at Makasa, that city defending the western approach to Kampala, just as Jinja defends the east. Even now, I am told, they are slow in rebuilding Makasa. Marabou storks, those tall-legged birds that look all the same like vultures, wander in the ruins. Okello placed sniper nests forward of Makasa, deployed his small fleet of mobile recoilless rifles behind, and dug trenches as a third line of defence. There was not much mercy from the gentlemen of Nyerere. They pounded Okello for days, and then their tanks just rolled over any left to bar their way. Okello fled and has lived with himself as his own pariah ever since. Every night he dreams his body is laid out for the marabou storks to eat, pecked beakful by beakful. All the same, I wonder sometimes why we should put our trust in Alice. Is this now Okello desperate? But he says she, against all expectation, has some command of strategy – that, when he sits with her, he feels dialogues and conferences whistling in her head and that, if anyone arbitrates that convention of voices, it is her. I will not go with him to her. I am a soldier who has lived by simple killings. I abhorred the method of Amin. When it was my turn to kill, I did it swiftly, with economy. If the victim was brave, I would let him prepare himself. If he was weak, I would shoot him when he was unaware, and had no time for kneeling and pleading. Amin would make it slow. Not I, and not Okello; but the Maribou storks of his dreams never finish eating him, and I think he wants a finish. Either he will kill the nightmare birds, or he will walk towards the orphans' fussilade. This time, Okello will not run and, because of that, I follow Okello.

A young soldier in the government army

Since we came down from the Mountains of the Moon, there has only recently been rest for us. Now, we move into forward lines again before Jinja. How strange to defend a city rather than attack it. Although our officers say that we shall not defend at all, but move forward to attack as soon as we decipher the enemy formation. They plan to attack our defences, but we attack their disposition to attack. I understand this. It is to command psychological space. We are passing among ourselves books we have freed from the tight spaces of library shelves. There are copies of poems by Yeats. I am told a wild swan is like a white flamingo, only without the long legs and is as graceful in water as a flamingo is in flight. I understand this. There is a book on management, and this talks about commanding the space of the mind. If their mind thinks one thing, we shall do another. If their mind thinks it will take one action, we shall take that same action before they have even begun it. Thus, out-planned in their own plan, the enemy will lose confidence. These things are simple. We have been fighting like this since I was ten. Thus I give back the book on management and ask again for the poems by Yeats. These I do not fully understand, but I imagine certain understandings. Who was this woman he longed for? Does a man worship a woman like that? A strong woman like that? Even now, I understand little of women, I know nothing of other countries, I imagine flamingoes as swans, I imagine building a tower and living at its top, invulnerable and safe as white birds and pink birds wheel by – this Russian gun, with its safety catch filed off, at the bottom of the lake beside my tower. I shall have a bedroom at the very top, and greet visitors only at the bottom. No one will come to my room at the top; but I shall have a room with books, between bottom and top, and I shall ask only the fathers to visit me there – and we shall drink tea just as they like – and I shall ask them to explain to me this poet, Yeats. And ask them if I am right, when I see Alice's army, an army I shall fight to destroy, that this is like the beast that slouches towards Bethlehem. Is this truly the army of God? And, if it is, am I right to fight it? And, if it is not the army of God, does not even Uganda deserve the attention of God? For we have seen Museveni and know he is good, but he is no saviour – but I look at the army of Alice, and I must see no saviour; and, when I fight, those I fight will see no salvation. This gun has killed many. Tomorrow, it is destined to kill many. But I have sworn, on my heart and to my dead mother, it will never kill a swan or a flamingo. When I see the flamingos fly, away from the salt and sulphur lakes where they stand, when I see them fly free, I think of my mother and father. Then I think that Amin's soldiers are hidden within Alice's army. Tomorrow, I shall kill everyone who stands before me.

An officer reporting to Museveni

They are deployed well, behind two wedge formations, with three squares behind each wedge. The centre square in each case contains the experienced soldiers. They will clearly seek to follow behind the charismatics who will throw themselves at us. They have two squares of lesser charismatics flanking them, nothing behind them – so they can retreat in an orderly fashion if all goes badly. They clearly seek to risk as little as possible, but will sacrifice any number of the charismatics. About one in three of the frontline charismatics carries a discernibly modern rifle. They have a smattering of older hunting rifles and some pistols. The lesser charismatics who protect the flanks of the soldiers carry only a very few rifles of any description, but are armed mostly with rocks and clubs and staves. Several of them carry elaborate wire models of aircraft and some tanks. These will make living room souvenirs, but it is a shame – for they imagine that Alice has power inside her head to transform the wire models into actual aircraft and tanks. This, sir, is what they imagine their armour to be. Some of the senior officers of the soldiers ride in Land Cruisers, and one or two of these have mounted machine guns. Alice, herself, rides to battle on a bicycle. The charismatics are covered in oil and prepare by chanting magic formulae. These seem like a cross between hymns and obscure Acholi invocations to the spirit world. It seems they hope themselves to be flanked by a regiment of ancestors who will have angels' wings. Even if their aircraft do not materialize, the angel ancestors will glide above them and command the skies, and lacerate our positions.

Sir, the chanting may well demoralize our own soldiers. Not all of them have completed their literacy training, and they have only ever faced secular enemies. We must send the priests among them to tell them that the faith of the charismatics is false. Also, assuming the charismatics chant all night, we should attack just before dawn – they will be tired, their chanting will be subdued, and they will not see us coming. We have drawn up a plan to send two mobile columns forward, one on either side of the outer flanking squares, drive them in upon the trained soldiers, not let them arrange themselves as they had hoped. Each of our Land Cruisers has either Browning machine guns mounted, or a recoilless rifle. They have enough ammunition to keep up a steady fire into the ranks of the lesser charismatics. The frontline wedges will still come forward, but without the full weight of soldiers following behind. Sir, we recommend that we let them make some progress, let them become confident and careless; we need to see their formation lose its compactness; they have to become careless with the ease of their charging forward, and lose the concentrated spearhead of their push upon our lines. We have arranged machine-gun nests in a staggered zigzag formation. They will open fire in strict order: the forward nests will fire first. The charismatics will think we have no guns in the gaps and fall forward towards those gaps. When they do that, the second tier of guns will open fire. When they rush to retreat, they will fall upon their comrades, and the soldiers will be enveloped by their own wedge and flanking cannon fodder.

What if they break through both tiers of machine-gun nests? Sir, we have no further lines of defence. All I can say is that not many of the enemy will be in any fit state to march on Kampala. All of Uganda will be settled here in Jinja – fate and future – and it will be, sir, a future of either you as president, or the advent of Magic. How shall we explain Her to the world? Even so, what can we say even of ourselves? When we grouped and trained in the Mountains of the Moon, did not some kind of magic light wash away the years of defeat and timidity? Did we not feel that everything would be possible? Who knows, Sir, if this is not the test of magic armies – and will it be moon-fed victors, or the triumph of Alice and the forces of the Holy Spirit?

A Tanzanian observer with Museveni's army

These deployments, theirs and ours, are so like those of 200 years ago. At least the boys have guns, and will not be mown down playing fife and drums. Those who will be mown down will be Alice's people. Whoever heard of an army carrying toys it hopes will change into weapons? We all accept that, beyond a certain point, we should cease our own firing and take no reprisals. Enough savagery from this part of the world already. Unless, that is, I am very much mistaken and Alice breaks through. What will she commit in Kampala? And if commit no atrocity, what will she do with the civil service, with the university? What will her army do when it sees the thousands of books at Makerere, the long row of new files that suddenly follows on from old and dusty files in the basement of parliament? Will we see this Alice, dressed in French couture, fly to New York to address the United Nations? Will she wear perfumes and shake the hands of ambassadors and presidents? Eat with nicety and govern with nicety? It is intriguing, I grant you that. I grant you a rueful sentimentality: that Africa should, even now, emit the possibility of perfumed witch in the wake of medieval tyranny. At least the armies ape Wellington and Napoleon's – they are, I venture, a little closer to the times that truly oppress us.

Alice on the eve of battle

Looking out towards Jinja, I feel I am looking out from a balcony – something high above. Like the balcony of King David in the Mormon books. There is a quarrel within my head as I look out but it is I, Alice, who gathered this army together; it is me the army sees; it does not see the high command within. This part of me who remains me wonders indeed about the magic oils, the chants and rituals of invulnerability, the wire aircraft that shall become flying steel, the rocks that will become grenades as we throw them. But will the army of Museveni fire upon these unarmed men and women? I have buried the soldiers of Amin deep within our formations – so they will be unable to fire upon the enemy. It is time we stopped being enemies. Allow us a march into Kampala, and I shall reconcile the broken nation with true beliefs and pure judgements. I shall summon a different council of spirits from all tribes of Uganda, and rule with them inside this spacious head. We shall perform the rituals of all people, and there will be a code of laws that allows each law to speak to another. But I distrust the army of Museveni. They will fire on us. And I distrust our spells of protection. I ask, therefore, that the ancestral spirits of the Acholi become great clouds of dust, great clouds of enveloping dust, and that they wrap us as we advance, and blind the eyes of all before us. I ask that spirits and flesh become one storm. I ask that I, as vortex, calmly invade Kampala.

Ching Po from within Alice

If the spirits rise as dust, the enemy will still fire into the dust. It is for us to attack too swiftly for them to respond with the carnage of their weapons. Some 80 years ago, outside the gates of Peking, did I not see this very same situation? Did I not lead then an army of oiled and almost naked men, chanting invulnerabilities as, swords in hand, they charged the bullets and cannon of an enemy?

This being oiled and naked, and believing magic – this is

sometimes the only way to rise. For, from time to time, Heaven says 'rise'; or something inside you says 'rise'; and there is nothing with which to rise. And, before you, are armies with a phalanx of weapons that say 'you cannot rise'. And you say you will nevertheless rise. It is an innocent word, this 'nevertheless', but in some ways it is the most powerful word in all languages. In Chinese, in Swahili, in what the Acholi speak. And it is not I or Alice who say 'rise'. Alice simply said, 'why not rise?', and the Acholi nation said 'we will rise'. It was then that the spirits came to Alice, for saying 'rise' alone cannot bring victory or protection. The spirits said there were weapons to face the weapons of the government. But we are spirits, and the weapons we bring are weapons of the spirit.

The dust spirits whom Alice now brings are of a lesser order. Alice conceives of them as ancestors, but they are only the spirits of dust. Their role is to animate dust. Our role is to animate Alice, but then be arbitrated by her. The act of possession is also an act of acceptance that we have entered a preformed being. But Alice understands when I speak of the gates of Peking; she understands thunderbolts that come from the palms of magicked men; she does not ask why the thunderbolts did not come at Peking; she sees Jinja, and she knows that thunderbolts may come; if they do not come, she still sees Jinja. She understands objectives; she understands safety, so she has buried the murderous soldiers of Amin deep within the magic ranks; and she understands that the government army will stand and fight, and that is why she summons the dust spirits – they are her contingency when thunderbolts fail to fall. We asked for storms at Peking, but the white garrison stood behind walls. What is it that Museveni's men stand behind? The dust may help, but we had better be swift.

The leader of the dust spirits

As if we were only spirits of dust, pure and simple. We hear
the Greek gods sent dreams to the kings of men. Each dream
was a spirit. Together they were only the spirits of dreams.
This word 'only' – we shall be dust that is here decisive, and
dust that is as complex as dreams.

Watch us now at Jinja. Alice summoned us, but it is we who
shall shape ourselves – now swirls, now blasts, now dust that
hangs like fog. Now tall, and now aimed at the eyes, now
punctuated by light, then blotting out the sun. If this battle
starts at dawn, for many the sun will never rise.

The king of the marabou storks

We are summoned by the dreams of Okello. The time has
come to end dreams. When dreams become reality, the time of
dreams has ended. We shall fly above the battle. Perhaps the
fighters will think we are spirits. No, we have simply flown in
from Kampala, where we perch on the tall building called
Parliament. We shall escort to Parliament whoever wins this
battle. But we shall first eat, while the fallen fighters rest.

One of those who fell at Peking, and who has haunted Ching Po since

The boys dream of flamingoes and swans, the storks dream of
banquets, the dust dreams of being dreams, Okello dreams of
ending dreams, Ching Po dreams of Peking. This *mélange*,
when even Ugandan dust can talk in Greek, and several
nations are convened in one woman's head, and commanders –
trained or magicked – talk of Jinja as if it were Waterloo, is
mélange indeed. Or more menagerie inside that Alice head. I

am not permitted entrance to that head. Among the circling spirits I am alone not here to fight – though I will relive my fight – and all the conversations inside Alice are overheard by all those overhead: spirits, storks, dust that shapes itself into mirage jets.

To stand before a defended city, guns indicating your own oiled body, and you give an incantation in reply, sword in hand and speech on lips – you are naked apart from sword and speech; and you are told to go forward, sword following speech, speech following a grammar you have memorized, memory based on rituals, rituals drawn from older times, those times declared ancestral, ancestors having turned their losses and defeats into new paeans of praise for rituals, so you do not know if the rituals are to exonerate the ancestors or to protect yourself, but you go forward because the guns aimed at your body are guns that would, in any case, be aimed against your body; only now you come to them, excising the future when they will come to you. And that is what you excise – the future. For guns speak and your speech ends, and Ching Po knows this, and he does not stop five thousand Acholi speeches, and tomorrow dawn the speeches and the dreams will go forward.

Alice on the dawn of battle

There are 1000 each in the two forward wedge formations. Each forward formation is followed by three columns of 500 each. The central column in each case is composed of Okello's men. Thus, 1000 soldiers and 4000 followers of Alice. A squadron of dust spirits. An increasingly large high command now sits within my head. I should say I am heavy-headed as we await the start of it all, but I wish to say instead I am lighthearted. The mixture of Heaven is this mixture we have assembled on earth. Win or lose today, this mixture will seep into every crevice. But I wish it not merely to be seepage. I wish a fountain in Kampala, and all nations will come and drink at this fountain. A great spirit will emerge and say, 'come', and take me as His bride, and thus fulfil the prophecy. But, before that, we must win today's fight. Yet, let it be won by those who believe in Alice, not those who believed in Amin. Okello is bitter and his men are savage. But they must be the hidden spine of this beast slouching forward. I simply rather they do not become its claws. But every man and woman who carries a rifle has filed away the safety catch. When shooting starts it will start with the lightest touch, a gentle pressure inwards. The finger must behave differently to the stomach – which will tighten and tremble in every fighter. But let the stomach move the finger to pull too hard and the rifle will spray its cargo upwards, and only birds will fall, and dust become despirited. The dust is thickening now, swirling in the branches, along the road, some sticking to the oiled bodies of the fighters. I see Okello in his Land Cruiser, instructing his officers; he has put on sunglasses against the dust; they have all put on sunglasses against the dust. But I can see through the dust, in the same way as any man sees through spirit. When your eyes are trained, you can see or not see as you choose. It was I who chose to be chosen as Alice, to see spirits when I wished, to gather spirits when the nation needed, who arranged the formations like Wellington, but who invited Ching Po to make best use of fighters most unlike those whom Wellington stacked in the field.

When I, Alice, mount my bicycle and move forward, all the 5000 will move forward. Some 400 metres from here, they will start to run; 500 metres and the shouting and incantations will start; at 1000 metres the forward wedges will begin to fire their weapons. We advance across a four-kilometre front. We anticipate the enemy will be spread too thin to stop us, yet we have enough depth and weight following behind to break through. And, if we are slowed, there are always the soldiers of Amin who are, effectively, the second wave – though I hope that wave will not be needed. Ching Po says that we shall lose 1000 fighters, one half of the forward formations. But all of this rests upon the enemy fighting from defensive positions outside Jinja. What if they come forward? In what way would they come forward? In what way could they now see what it is they move towards? For dust is high, and dust moves forward, and it is time now for Alice and the 5000 to move forward, and God bless us and recognize His own Holy Spirit Whom I have asked to move forward.

An aide to Okello

God help us now. She has given the signal to advance. Those of us in Land Cruisers will move very slowly at first, give space to those marching and running before. At least neither side has artillery or aircraft. It will not be massacre from the skies but, as from time immemorial, it will be front to front, shock and absorb. If this formation cannot absorb the shock, then no formation can. Then we shall strike as the second shock and the government lines will break. I tell you, I shall shed this uniform when we enter Kampala. I shall dine as a victorious normal man dines – and that will not be a camouflaged man; a man of many killings; a man who has lived in border enclaves; but a man who lifts a glass like any man. It will be a naked and free lifting of a glass, and I shall not get drunk, I shall see the world through this glass and see the reflection of me seeing the world, and that will be enough. Even if some relative of some man I have killed comes behind me then, claims his blood debt, I shall be satisfied because of that free moment.

A Tanzanian observer

It is starting. They come with dust. They have called upon their dusty gods. Here, there are the usual chatterings of teeth, one or two puddles staining uniforms, but no one leaves his position. Those who lead the flanking counterattack are getting ready now. In a very real sense, our lives depend on them. Once hypnotized by their own spells, the charismatics will have no discrimination when they start to kill. Blood lust will come early to them, and even a rock that does not explode can still be used to pound a skull. To be shot will be at least to die cleanly. But how they come – their great noise behind their storm of dust and, overhead, strange birds fly with them.

The king of the marabou storks

We fly now. Even if Alice's wire planes never rise as hardened steel, we fly. But we do not fly only for her. We fly because the voyeurs and feasters upon death fly. But we are, in our own way, fastidious. Being long-legged means our plumage will not be bloodstained by the remains of men. This seems macabre, yes? But it is not we who kill. It is we who observe those who kill, and it is our reward to feed, and it is our task to escort the columns that emerge victorious from the blood mêlée. For, atop one of the seven hills, there is indeed that prize called Parliament. Those who sit and speak debate the fate of peoples. We decide no fates. We talk little, observe much. Now, as we fly, we observe the armies of men. We too, like Alice, can see through dust and spirits, and we see now Museveni's two mobile columns leave Jinja – to envelop Alice just as she hoped dust would envelop sight of her advance. And Alice, who sees through dust, cannot see through the thousands of her own fighters, and does not see the threat that will rain upon her sides – she who thought so carefully about her push-through from the front. And those of us who fly and see through dust, we see what guns these columns carry; and, unless dust thickens even more – but dust is dancing like our dreams – there will be slaughter in an hour; Okello's men will turn and run, killing their own allies to cut a pathway out; but Okello, we know, will this time stand and fight. No bullet will cut him down, but running feet; and all his insignia will be trampled into earth. But it is not we who will feast upon Okello. Those who fly above us say that dust will carry him to his own land. They say great chivalries will be paid at the end of the day, and the orphans will play with the wire planes, and they will watch Alice ride away, and Museveni will hang no man who struck against him this hot and dusty day.

The prince of flamingoes in his sulphur lake

We hear of a great battle and great slaughters two days' flight away. The skies have their own song lines, and so this news is sung, our laws being that the darker the news the more melodic the song. Throughout Uganda, all birds know it, all long-legged birds know it and step differently in acknowledgement. Secretary birds step more delicately, we ourselves change the pattern of our standing, even the marabou storks knew it decent to pause in their incessant pecking.

The world of flamingoes knows the news. In Ethiopia they predict the convening of presidents to hear Museveni. They will not hear Alice who, even now, limps away from battle, still wheeling her bicycle. A silent convention of marshals is limping with her, hanging low her head with the down tread of every second step.

It is in Addis that we flamingoes once sought to provoke the world of international relations. When Michaelangelo boasted he would gift the Emperor of Abyssinia with a painting, it was a flamingo that travelled from Addis and appeared before him, saintly and glossy, one day in the Pope's own chambers, and offered to carry the gift. It sits still in that Addis chapel they built above the remains of emperors. When men boast, and when men war, it is carried on the song lines and we, who do not have to thud the earth without respite, can wheel in the air to mourn calamity and shattered hopes and blasted families. For many have begun to cry in Uganda this day, and there are many who, having lost their parents, now join them – some carrying books of poetry and muttering final lines before a rock exploded among them. For Alice's people almost broke through in their thrust forward, before collapsing inwards. Many rocks exploded, for a moment it seemed a squadron of planes flew overhead. Great clouds of dust wrapped everything and a choir was heard in the distance, even above the tumult of war, a choir singing Catholic hymns. A gentleman from Tanzania was struck speechless, before a rock also struck him.

Still there are echoes on the battlefield – Misereres and Te Deums – as the Marabou convention, with occasional pause and restraint, began its work. And Museveni's victors wonder how much was vision and how much real, but their men and boys are many among the dead and, even now, friends pick among the bodies, hoping to rescue loved ones from the storks and the stench, all those who came together in the Mountains of the Moon, and all the time of magic is over now for Uganda.

Secularized Alice in the marketplace

But, you see, everything worked as we had planned it to work. It is just that we did not plan to see their plan. All that spiritual energy to direct the beast forward – you cannot change its direction in an instant. All night I had been building mass from my energy, and it was all directed forward. We would have broken through. They could not have blunted the sword's thrusting tip, but they snapped the sword in two.

As we retreated, my head kept dropping to one side. I realized then that all in the high command were limping, though attempting a military march. Soon, I was not merely pushing my bicycle, but leaning upon it for support. When we knew we were not being pursued, I stopped and someone helped me repair the chain, but I knew I could not ride if my head were weighted to one side. I asked if my friends could balance themselves in some central space. After all, the head is large and spirits can make themselves small. But they said, no, they had come to Uganda to grow, not to become small, and they came out of my head and I saw them sit with me by a well. I sat under a tree, but they said that spirits have no need of shade, and they were all very handsome – as you expect spirits to be, having corrected the blemishes of lives long ago – and their voices very harmonious. They would take, thank you, no water – this with much courtesy and thanks to my kind hosting and clean accommodation – but wanted one last conversation before they set off. There would be other lands in need of magic.

For spirits are themselves victims, or those who have failed in a grand enterprise. Perhaps I myself shall be a spirit, searching for the grand success. I felt sorry for them. For Ching Po it was like the gates of Peking – only this time he almost got it right. The Congolese spirit said he too was sorry, yet not sorry. He said there is no pure past for Africa, and it is not this past from which the future must spring. He said the future is the careful ordering of influences and preferences. The influences jostle in the past, the preferences are our choices for the future. He said that Africa is to be composed – one part hymn, one part ululation. And one part science – here the American spirit spoke. The preferences, he said, must marry science and its rationalities with the different rationalities of past and present cultures. A culture is nothing abstract, but must live pragmatically. A culture is squeezed, and survives only through flexibility. The Italian spoke. Of them all, he was oldest and wisest. He had built bridges and roads in a former life. He looked down the road to Jinja – beyond it the straight route to Kampala – and said that we should never have gone down the straight roads, but taken several winding paths towards Kampala. We should have been impossible to find and fight, until we sprang up severally inside the capital itself. But this, he said, takes even greater planning than a straight road. And a host of latter-day marshals, who had found their way into my head, agreed that the plans had been too formal – but drawn, they said, from the dawn of Europe's own modernity. Was not Napoleon the consolidator of citizens and the bequeather of constitutions? So I looked at these marshals, and wondered which ones had been with Napoleon. He was said to have surrounded himself only with young commanders. One had been almost girlish, tender skin needing face creams, and long hair needing hats with plumes and ribbons. He would change his coat several times during battle, to sparkle in the mud or dust. But he was contemptuous of death and had commanded cavalry. How he must have wished for horses at Jinja – not a prophetess who rode forward on a bicycle.

So, we said goodbye at the well and they became light, and the rays flew off in different directions, some singly and some as proven friends together. When I stood, my head was no longer heavy and I no longer limped; my bicycle had been repaired; I had a last insight of the sort that spirits bring – hearing Museveni's officers far away, receiving orders to let me and my Holy Spirit Army go. I thought to go to Kenya, then thought to remain in Uganda. I had small gardens where tomatoes, rape and bananas grew. I would become Alice who sold these things in a clean market, and sufficient people would know me as I was, and my message would go forth in silent circles of private acknowledgement.

The speaker of the parliament of flamingoes in Ethiopia

In Addis, some few miles north, the presidents of Africa gather. Their great planes are flying overhead, bringing comfortable men with many papers. Their hotel is set in gardens and the gardens are surrounded by dusty streets and the fumes of endless cars. In the city trees, eagles sit and, each evening, wheel about the city. From their formations we understand the debates of each chambered and besuited day. The presidents congratulate Museveni, and make jokes about a witch president that, thankfully, never was. When they sip whisky, they toast the small man from Uganda – and he, himself, begins to forget those Mountains of the Moon where he also felt magic and the impulse to go forth. For when men rebel and go forth, do they first not need to taste light, and have light enter their fevered heads? It is light that clarifies, and it is light that carries spirits and creatures that do not die as easily as the men and women they once were. Museveni forgets this as he takes his drink. The presidents slap his back and shake his hand, and he is used now to fine cloth upon his back and, like a bird who preens his plumage, forgets sometime the need to fly.

Birds of the Parliament, perhaps Alice should have broken through. What would the proud Kenyans and prouder Tanzanians have done then? What greetings would be given from presidents here in Addis? How quickly would she have learnt their ways? How quickly would she have learnt not to appear ridiculous to the world? For the world would have found her ridiculous, but Alice may well have understood the world better than these presidents who talk with learning on their tongues, and less learning in their thoughts. Who should tell? And what is it to the kingdoms and domains of birds? But that, once, spirits and ghost planes flew over Jinja – and someone called a witch almost became the president of Uganda.

Bibliography

Achebe, Chinua (1987) *Anthills of the Savannah*, London: Heinemann

Amado, Jorge (1984) *The Violent Land*, London: Collins Harvill

Bayat, Jean Francois (1989) *L'état en Afrique: la politique du ventre*, Paris: Fayard

Behrend, Heike (1999) *Alice Lakwena and the Holy Spirits: War in Northern Uganda 1986–7*, London: James Currey

Blyden, Edward W. (1994) *Christianity, Islam and the Negro Race*, Baltimore: Black Classic

Chabal, Patrick (1986) *Political Domination in Africa: Reflections on the Limits of Power*, Cambridge: Cambridge University Press

Chabal, Patrick and Jean-Pascal Daloz (1999) *Africa Works: Disorder as Political Instrument*, Oxford: James Currey

Chan, Stephen (2002) *Composing Africa: Civil Society and its Discontents*, Tampere: Tampere Peace Research Institute

Clarke, Roy (2004) *The Worst of Kalaki*, Lusaka: Bookworld

Commission for Africa (2005) *Our Common Interest: Report of the Commission for Africa*, London: Commission for Africa

Conrad, Joseph (1994) *Heart of Darkness*, London: Penguin Classics

Cruise O'Brien, Donal (2003) *Symbolic Confrontations: Muslims Imagining the State in Africa*, London: Hurst

Dasgupta, Partha (1995) *An Enquiry into Well-Being and Destitution*, Oxford: Clarendon

Decalo, Samuel (1976) *Coups and Army Rule in Africa: Studies in Military Style*, New Haven: Yale University Press de Waal, Alex (1989) *Famine that Kills: Darfur, Sudan, 1984–5*, Oxford: Clarendon

Drayton, Richard (2006 forthcoming) *The Caribbean and the Making of the Modern World,* no place: no publisher

Ellis, Stephen (1999) *The Mask of Anarchy: The Destruction of Liberia and the Religious Dimension of an African Civil War*, London: Hurst

Ellis Stephen and Gerrie ter Haar (2004) *Worlds of Power: Religious Thought and Political Practice in Africa*, Oxford: Oxford University Press

Fanon, Frantz (1965) *The Wretched of the Earth*, New York: Grove

(1986) *Black Skin, White Masks*, London: Pluto

Finer, S. E. (1975) *The Man on Horseback: The Role of the Military in Politics*, London: Penguin

First, Ruth (1970) *The Barrel of a Gun: Political Power in Africa and the Coup d'Etat*, London: Allen Lane

Gutteridge, William (1975) *Military Regimes in Africa*, London: Methuen

Hatch, John (1976) *Two African Statesmen*, London: Secker & Warburg

Huntington, Samuel P. (1957) *The Theory and Practice of Civil–Military Relations*, Cambridge, Mass: Harvard University Press

Hove, Chenjerai (1988) *Bones*, Harare: Baobab

Iliffe, John (1987) *The African Poor*, Cambridge: Cambridge University Press

Jeffries, Richard (1982) 'Rawlings and the Political Economy of Underdevelopment in Africa', *African Affairs*, vol. 81

Kanengoni, Alexander (1997) *Echoing Silences*, Harare: Baobab

Kirk-Greene, Anthony (1980) 'The Thin White Line: The Size of the Colonial Service in Africa', *African Affairs*, vol. 79

Kriger, Norma J. (1992) *Zimbabwe's Guerrilla War: Peasant Voices*, Cambridge: Cambridge University Press

Kwei Armah, Ayi (1969) *The Beautyful Ones Are Not Yet Born*, London: Heinemann

Longman, Timothy (1988) 'Rwanda: Chaos from Above', in Leonardo A. Villalon and Philip A. Huxtable (eds) *The African State at a Critical Juncture*, Boulder Co: Lynne Rienner

Luckham, Robin (1994) 'The Military, Militarization and Democratization in Africa: A Survey of Literature and Issues', *African Studies Review*, vol. 37

Macey, David (2000) *Frantz Fanon: A Biography*, New York: Picador

Mills, Greg (2002) *Poverty to Prosperity: Globalisation, Good Governance and African Recovery*, Johannesburg: Tafelberg

Mudimbe, Valentine (1988) *The Invention of Africa: Gnosis, Philosophy and the Order of Knowledge*, London: James Currey

Mugabe, Robert Gabriel (2001) *Inside the Third Chimurenga*, Harare: Department of Information and Publicity

Naipaul, V. S. (1980) *A Bend in the River*, Harmondsworth: Penguin

Patel, Preeti (2001) 'The Politics of AIDS in Africa', *International Relations*, vol. XV

Patocka, Jan (1981) *Essais heretiques sur la philosophie de l'histoire*, Lagrasse: Editions Verdier

Pelton, Robert D. (1980) *The Trickster in West Africa: A Study of Mythic Irony and Sacred Delight*, Berkeley: University of California Press

Poku, Nana and Fantu Cheru (2001) 'The Politics of Poverty and Debt in Africa's AIDS Crisis', *International Relations*, vol. XV

Ranger, Terence (1985) *Peasant Consciousness and Guerrilla War in Zimbabwe*, London: James Currey
(2005) 'The Uses and Abuses of history in Zimbabwe', in Mai Palmberg and Ranka Primorac (eds) *Skinning the Skunk: Facing Zimbabwean Futures*, Uppsala: Nordiska Afrikainstitutet

Rodney, Walter (1988) *How Europe Underdeveloped Africa*, London: Bogle l'Ouverture

Said, Edward W. (1993) *Culture and Imperialism*, London: Chatto & Windus

Sen, Amartya (1981) *Poverty and Famines: An Essay on Entitlement and Deprivation*, Oxford: Clarendon

Soyinka, Wole (1976) *Myth, Literature and the African World*, Cambridge: Cambridge University Press

Vail, Leroy (1989) (ed) *The Creation of Tribalism in Southern Africa*, London: James Currey

Vargas Llosa, Mario (1985) *The War of the End of the World*, London: Faber & Faber

van Dong, Jan Kees (1995) 'Zambia', in John Wiseman (ed) *Democracy and Political Change in Sub-Saharan Africa*, London: Routledge

Vera, Yvonne (2002) *The Stone Virgins*, Harare: Weaver

wa Thiong'o, Ngugi (1977) *Petals of Blood*, Harare: Zimbabwe Publishing House
(1987) *Decolonising the Mind*, Harare: Zimbabwe Publishing House

Williams, Raymond (1973) *The Country and the City*, London: Chatto & Windus

Young, Crawford (1994) *The African Colonial State in Comparative Perspective*, New Haven: Yale University Press

Zartman, I. William (1995) (ed.) *Collapsed States: The Disintegration and Restoration of Legitimate Authority*, London: Lynne Rienner

Zolberg, Aristotle (1968) 'The Structure of Political Conflict in the New States of Tropical Africa', *American Political Science Review*, vol. LXII

Index